COMING UP TO LIGHT

By:

Dr. Gene Herndon

AiON MULTIMEDIA
"The Word is Eternal" Isaiah 40:8

Printed in the United States of America

Published by Aion Multimedia
20118 N 67th Ave
Suite 300-446
Glendale AZ 85308
www.aionmultimedia.com

ISBN-13: 9780997604603

TABLE OF CONTENTS

Table of Contents

UNDERSTANDING LIGHT

"This, then, is the message which we have heard of him, and declare unto you, that God is light, and in him is no darkness at all. If we say that we have fellowship with him, and walk in darkness, we lie, and do not the truth."
—*1 John 1:5-6*

"Light" in the Bible is a reference to revelation or to clarity and understanding. You can't be judged on things you don't know. When you bring a lot of light, you position yourself to garner an immense amount of attack and you put yourself right on the front line. The Bible does not say that we *say not* the truth, it says we *do not* the truth. What you say is a reflection of what you believe. By faith, you can say things that may not be current, but you are speaking it in a way that it will be. What makes it a lie is when you do what you are *not* saying. This brings hypocrisy.

"And on the morrow, when they were come from Bethany, he was hungry. And seeing a fig tree afar off, having leaves, he came, if haply he might find any thing on it, and when he came to it, he found nothing but leaves; for the time of figs was not yet. And Jesus answered and said unto it, No man eat fruit of thee hereafter forever. And his disciples heard it."
—*Mark 11:12-14*

It seems like a very bizarre thing when He said He answered it. Jesus answered a tree! If you understand the growth of fruit and vegetables, as the sun hits them they change color.

Anything that is a dark blue, purple, or green has to typically grow without direct exposure to sunlight. A fig tree that has leaves on it should have figs, because the leaves come out first, and then figs grow underneath. Jesus is excited because He saw the leaves. He comes to the tree knowing that the tree has leaves, which means it should have fruit. From the outside it looks like it's a productive and producing plant, but when He gets up to further inspection, it has no fruit. This story is not about a tree; it's about hypocrisy. It's about saying one thing and doing another. It's about having the appearance, but not having real fruit. It's about saying "I'm a Christian" but living like Satan.

God hates hypocrisy. That's why He said, "I rather you be hot or cold" (Revelation 3:15). People will say, *"Well you know, Pastor, God's working on me."* You know what that is, right? That's Christianese loosely translated to, *"I refuse to change so I'm just going to say God's working on me which licenses me to act a fool a little longer."* You have to be careful because you can almost give yourself permission to walk in darkness. You can almost give yourself license to do darkness because the world is dark.

Unfortunately, we tend to think because some things become our pet sin that it's not that bad. *At least I'm not a crack head. So-and-so lives like this... I'm not as bad as them.*

First of all, the Bible says that he who compares themselves among themselves, that group is just not wise (2 Corinthians 10:12). In that level of comparison, you dumb down your sins, your iniquities, and your inabilities, thinking, *"It's okay that I look the part. I can find a nice suit and nice clothes. I can get in church and act like I'm holy, wave my hands and go through all of the gestures and speak the rhetoric of Christendom."* However, you can't walk it out in your life. You struggle to apply the Word in all areas of your life; therefore, because you can't apply it to all areas of your life, you have a form of godliness but deny the power thereof (see 2 Timothy 3:5). You can *look* the part, but you can't *walk* the part. You can come into church and love everybody at church, smile and act nice, then go home and talk about them. The fruit is not there.

See, there's no darkness in God at all. So if the story of the fig tree is about hypocrisy, what Jesus is saying is that He cursed it so that it could not produce—because it refused to produce. Jesus did not curse a perfectly healthy tree and say, "Now you can't produce." What He did was give words to its behavior. If it were to produce fruit, the fruit would have been there when He showed up. However, when He showed up, because it had no fruit He said, "You're cursed and no man will ever eat from you again." Some people will say Jesus was angry because He was hungry, but it says He was haply going. He wasn't angry; He became angry when He realized the tree was a hypocrite; He realized that the tree looked like a Christian but it was not. It had the form of Christianity, but it had no fruit of Christianity; it was hypocrisy at its highest level.

"And these things write we unto you, that your joy may be full. This, then, is the message which we have heard of him, and declare unto you, that God is light, and in him is no darkness at all. If we say that we have fellowship with him, and walk in darkness, we lie, and do not the truth: But if we walk in the light, as he is in the light, we have fellowship one with another, and the blood of Jesus Christ, his Son, cleanseth us from all sin. If we say that we have no sin, we deceive ourselves, and the truth is not in us. If we confess our sins, he is faithful and just to forgive us our sins, and to cleanse us from all unrighteousness."
—1 John 1:4-9

Our fellowship with one another comes through Him. As a believer, the only way you can fellowship with another believer is you both have to be in Him to have real fellowship. In Him there is no darkness or ulterior motive. You do not come to church looking for your future spouse, your boyfriend or girlfriend; looking to have sex with people or with impure motives. If you are in Him and they are in Him, then His purpose will prevail in your life and fruit will become what light is—which light is not in darkness. You do not go to church looking to make a profit. *I came because I need some business connections.* That's not what you go for. When you come with the right purpose and motive, you cannot have fellowship with one another unless you have fellowship with Christ, and to have fellowship with Him is to walk in light. When you walk in light, you have a purpose in light. Light will cause you to see things differently and to fellowship one with another based on the things of God and not on the things of your flesh. When you come with real motives and real intentions, God reigns supreme in your life. All you want is more of God and when you seek after that—not ulterior motives—then you come together with other believers and have real fellowship.

John says, "If you walk in the light as he is in the light..." (1 John 1:7). This tells me that I can walk in different places and still be in the same spot. Just because people walk into the church does not mean they walk in the light. I could drink diesel, smoke like a chimney, and sleep in a garage, but that doesn't make me a truck. I don't think I'd live very long, but I could do it. As Christ is in the light, we all may have different degrees of light, but it's all the same kind of light. It all comes from the same place.

Each person may have a different level of light. I don't listen to secular music, and some people might say that's just too much. That's the light they walk in. I can't be listening to Jay-Hovah, and come into the church to preach a message. I have to be listening to THE Jehovah. If you are aspiring to the deeper things with God, then you're going to have to learn to fine-tune your ears. First of all, music was originated by God. The perversion of music is an entrance point into your life. It used to be a day where the songs were talking about love, getting married; there was a different type of thing going on. Now it's like *"kill 'em, shoot 'em, stab 'em, sleep with 'em, roll around with 'em, smoke it, snort it, smack it, flip it..."*

Here's the childishness; *"I can listen to what I want to because I know the difference."* However, even the music that's Christian isn't necessarily Christian. A lot of what is labeled as Christian is sung by people who couldn't make it secularly and they just changed the words. It used to be, *"Hold me and kiss me and give me sloppy wet kisses, Jimmy."* Then they took Jimmy out and put God in there. If I want to give you something to remember, then I can do a couple of things that make everything planted deeper into your mind. "I before E except after C unless sounding like A as in neighbor and weigh." We were all taught that as kids, but it's not always true. Why did we learn it? Because it rhymes. I set it to music. If I set it to music, I can implant it.

I have a light I walk in that you may not walk in. There are things I can do that you might not understand, and things I cannot do that might not make any sense to you, but that's the light I walk in. The problem is the Bible tells us that for him who knows it's sin and does it, that's sin to him (James 4:17).

I can choose to be in the light, or I can choose to walk in darkness. It's the same path, but I can choose which way I want to go. I can walk in the flesh (the darkness), or I can walk in the light.

The higher you go with God, the more He expects. It's one thing when you first get in; you have your baby bottle and blankey and it's just great. However, as you mature, God weans you away from the things that have become crutches for you. He wants you to depend upon Him. He wants you to walk in the light. As you walk in the light, you now have fellowship.

Often when we hear the word "fellowship," do we think about what that means? The Greek word for fellowship is *koinonia* which means face-to-face—the position a man and a woman who are married find themselves in with their covenant. Childish people think sex is just sex; adults, when they grow up, put away childish things and realize they cannot put themselves in those types of predicaments because they're too old for that stuff. We realize that it means more when we lie face-to-face with somebody.

If we understand fellowship, and we understand that God wants to fellowship with us, we know He is saying, "When I get face-to-face with you, I'm going to take care of you. I'm going to love you and do whatever I can to take care of you." Real face-to-face means all of those things because God said, "When I fellowship with you, I cannot be any more intimate with you. I'm your supply, I'm your deliverer. I am face-to-face intimate with you. No one else will come between us because I am the One who will take care of you."

See now, the higher you go, the more you're required to understand what is light. Let's say you saw a 35-year-old at work, and the boss comes in and tells that 35-year-old, "We're not going to go with your idea." If they jump up, fall on the ground, start kicking, screaming, and crying, you would wonder, *What is their problem? Who does that?* Now here's the question: Why do you not understand that in the spirit, you're expected to grow up just as you are in the physical? The problem is that physically you can be as old as Methuselah, but in the spirit you can be a baby. How do you know which one you are? Do you throw temper tantrums in the spirit? Let me tell you what a spiritual temper tantrum looks like: *Why God? Why not? How come You won't...? I wish You would...*

A spiritually mature person says, "God, I know You have perfect timing. I'm going to sit here and be patient. I'm not going for Mrs. Right Now, I'm going for Mrs. Right. I'm going to wait until the right one comes. I'm not going to every Tom, Dick and Harry." That's patience; that's understanding God's timing. *Where's my money? Where are my finances? My money is funny!* Your money is funny because your confession is funny. Maturity will cause you to speak things and then act appropriately. Then if you speak it, say it, and do it, you're not lying. Now we know you have fellowship because what you say is what you do. You cannot be in the church acting like a Christian—raising your hands and worshipping like everybody else—and then sinning like the devil. God and Satan do not have fellowship with each other. You're either in the light or you're not in the light.

How do we get to a place where we understand that if He's in the light, then our protection comes in the light? When people begin walking in darkness, problems start happening. Their life flips around. Sometimes people's children start acting differently. But when the family gets back into the things of God, their children and their life straightens up.

Here's the childish part, however: They think God is the one who punished them. God is not punishing you; there's not a punishment bone in His body concerning you. Why would He give His only begotten Son for mankind to then beat you up? That does not make any sense. What has happened is that you made a decision to get out of the light and walk in darkness. Within darkness, Satan has every right to whoop your tail, which is why God said if you stay in fellowship with Him and you stay in the light, you save yourself healthy relationships. This is the difference between courting and dating. Courting is the intention of being married while dating is, *How do we get alone? How do I get her in dark places?* That's for two reasons: Nobody will know who it is, and you can do whatever you want to do. That's darkness.

When Billy Graham went into a city for a campaign, somebody would go into his hotel room prior to his arrival and check the closets and bathroom and then they would clear his room. Why? One time, they found somebody hiding in the closet with a camera, and a naked girl in the bed. They were waiting for him to walk in, the girl would then jump up, the photographer would come out of the closet, snap the shot, and Bingo! they've got him. Billy Graham said, "It's really hard to have sex with a woman if you're never alone with one."

This is walking in the light. With light comes wisdom and with wisdom comes understanding. Revelation is all about what you know. You cannot be somebody who doesn't understand the things of God but tries to walk in the things of God. The higher you go, the higher the expectation is of your life. If you are all about you, you'd better die. If you don't die, you'll get "kilt". Killed is what happens when it first occurs, "kilt" is when you are really dead.

It's not about you, it's about walking with Him. The closer you get to Him, the more successful your way becomes. Will you ever be perfect? No. I have to be careful when I say that because when I do, people substantiate their sinful life by saying, "I'm not perfect." When people say, "God's working on me," you know what they're saying? That's Christian rhetoric. That means, *The thing I know to deal with, I don't really want to, so I just say God is still working on me. That's an easy way for me to cop out and say I don't need to change.* How do we walk in light when there is no darkness in God at all?

This is what will cause pastors to be in positions as leaders over firecracker ministries. They move into position, build huge churches, then all of a sudden they are caught living promiscuously. Then we see it on TV and the whole church splits. Thousands and thousands of people are affected by it and you wonder, *How did God let that happen?* God *didn't* let that happen. This is what happens when man promotes man without the evidence of fruit; they're moved by what they say, not by what they do.

People say things like, "Pastor, I love you." You don't love me because you don't know me. My wife loves me; she knows me. None of you know me. What you love is my gift, and I'm okay with that as long as you keep it straight in your head and I keep it straight in mine. The moment I start thinking you love me and not my gift, I'll put more faith in me than the gift. The gift came from God. As long as you love God and walk in light, then we can have fellowship. When I walk in the light and you're in the light, we can have fellowship together and we can supply each other's needs when we walk in God. However, if we will not walk in God, the Bible says, "Can two walk together, except they be agreed?" (Amos 3:3). It's not possible for you to claim God and not walk with God. And it's impossible for you to quote God and not walk with God.

God is raising up some people that are about to get serious about His work. They're saying, "No! We're not going to live like this. We're not going to do this. We're going to walk in the light as He is in the light." When we do that, we see power.

You want to know why Christians have no power? It's not that God's mad at anybody; it's that they're not walking with God! How did we allow an agenda to shut the church down? We can't even talk about sexuality without it being labeled as hate speech. With the power of God behind us, how did 10 percent of the population shut the whole church down? We're not walking with God.

Darkness is dependent upon the absence of light. That means for me to walk in darkness, I have to shut off the light. People struggle because they shut off light in the areas of their life they do not want to deal with. Let's say it concerns money. Once you were at a place with your finances where you were walking in darkness. Now you've heard about tithing; it's been preached to you, you get it, you understand it, but you still refuse to tithe. In the area of your finances, the light goes out and in the darkness Satan can move. However, once I give my tithe, then suddenly the lights come on. Once I bring my offering, the lights come on.

If it's in the area of loving people, when I refuse to love, the lights go out. Now Satan can move because he is able to operate in darkness. However, once I realize I need to love my brother, the lights come on and in the light there is no darkness. The thing we tend to struggle with is the understanding that in God, there is no possibility of darkness. When light comes, it becomes a part of who we are. Jesus said as long as you walk in the light—not talk it, but do it—you produce fruit. Remember, He said it's not that we *say* not the truth, it's that we *do* not the truth. Isn't it funny how what we say is important, but it's not as important as what we do. It's what you do that will produce the fruit you need. God is the ultimate fruit inspector.

Revelation is when man hears what God says; inspiration is when man writes what God says; and illumination is when man receives that which was revealed and inspired. In other words, in all your getting, get understanding (see Proverbs 4:7). Kenneth Hagin Sr. said, "There are so many things that I want to teach you, but I can't." That's scriptural because Paul said the same thing. He said, "I'd like to tell you, but you're too carnal." People would ask Dad Hagin to record these words so they could listen to them later. He said, "You know that's not going to work because the first time you get out of my sight you're going to listen to it." Why did he say that? You would think that he'd rather not go to his grave with light and understanding that could have been a blessing for all of us.

I am careful what I teach. There are things I will not teach because once I teach it, you're responsible for it. You cannot be judged for what you don't know. If you don't know any better, how do I judge you? I have to be careful the amount of light and the type of light I bring. When I bring the light, you are now responsible once you've received it. This is why you have to be careful of the kind of light you allow to come into your life. Just because folks say they're Christian doesn't mean they are. Just because they can quote Scripture doesn't mean they know what Scripture says. Just because they know the Bible front and back does not mean they know the Bible front and back. You have to be very careful of the people you allow to speak into your life because not all light is of the right light. The Bible calls Satan an angel of light (2 Corinthians 11:14) because he can bring what appears to be light, but the truth of the matter is, it's darkness masquerading as light.

COMING UP TO LIGHT

"But the path of the just is like the shining light, that shineth more and more unto the perfect day."
—Proverbs 4:18

We know that perfect does not mean perfection; it's maturity. When you first start out, you might be walking in the fullness of light, but the path of the just should bring you to a place where you walk in more light. When you walk in more light, you qualify for more light. If you don't walk in the light you have, then stop looking for the light you won't walk in. God is a God of here a little there a little, line upon line, precept upon precept. He takes you step-by-step.

A guy came up to me in my old church and he said he couldn't pay his rent, that he was short a couple hundred bucks. He said, "What would you do?" I said, "You mean, what should *you* do?" He asked, "Isn't that the same thing?" I said, "No, it's not. I'll tell you what I would do. I'd take the four hundred dollars I have and I'd sow it into the church." I wasn't the pastor, I was just going to the church, but I had a revelation of money even then.

The reason some of you struggle with money is because you're too cheap with God. In one year my highest tithe was 50 grand. I know how to sow seed. The reason this man came to me and asked me is because he knew I was one of the most prosperous people in the church and wanted to know what I would do. I said, "You should figure out what *you* should do." I would just give it, but he didn't have the faith for that.

If you did what I would do, not having the light that I have, you would say one thing but not do the right thing. Now you'll walk in darkness and not in light because you'll say one thing but do another. You will give it and say you're in faith, but you'll freak out with what you do, which brings you to a place of incongruence with God.

As Kenneth Hagin would say, "A spiritual giant is one whose mind, spirit, and soul agree." When your heart and head are in total agreement, you are now a spiritual giant because anything is possible to them that believe (Mark 9:23). However, you must believe. I told the man to hold on to his money. When he walked away, another person asked me, "How come you didn't tell him to just sow it?" I said, "He didn't have the faith for it." How did I know he didn't have faith? he asked. What I have faith for, I'm not going to ask you.

Your opinion does not matter if I have faith. If I know it's God and I know He is going to bless me, then I'm going to do what He told me to do. I don't need to seek counsel from anyone else because I know my God is well able to do exceedingly, abundantly, more than I can ask or think (see Ephesians 3:20). So I am not moved by opinions of people; I'm moved by God's opinion. When I follow what He tells me to do, then I'm in the light with Him. Now I have fellowship with Him. There is no darkness in Him, so now everything I do, when I put my hands to it, will prosper. There's no incongruence between what I say and what I do. I don't plant a seed and then worry about it. If I write the check, I write the check. Glory to God, I know he's going to bless it. I say, "Father I thank You. Your word tells me that when I give, You will cause men to give unto me pressed down, shaken together and runneth over" (Luke 6:38). The measure in which I give it is the measure in which it comes back. So if it makes me nervous when I give it, it's going to bless me and make me nervous when I get it back! I understand it; I will not be deceived, and God is not going to be mocked. Whatever I sow, I will reap (see Galatians 6:7).

Then you have your childish people, *Well, it's not about this and that,* then stay struggling. In your head you're bringing glory to God. That's fine. Stay in the light you have. I was there. I was at that place where I said, "I'm not giving them my money. Uncle Sam takes about 28 percent, my wife takes half of it, then I give them 10 percent...dear God, there ain't much left!" I was there, but God forbid as the pastor I should not be there anymore. We are growing more and more, getting brighter and brighter unto the maturity of the perfect day. I will stand before Him and all will be revealed. I will have all the answers and I'll be clear. Until then, I'm supposed to grow.

People start serving God, right? Here's the thing: Depending on the level you start serving God in, it opens you up for an attack. What's funny is, the greatest attack comes from the people closest to you, from the ones who claim they love you. What they're mad about is the change in your relationship. Let's say a guy and girl have been dating for a while. She starts to attend church and becomes serious about the things of God. God is moving in her life, and now the guy wants to get married. He did not want to get married at all; he wasn't even thinking about getting married. Why does he now want to get married? He wants to lock her down. Vice versa, why does she want to marry? She wants to lock you down because now she's afraid that your relationship will change. *Well, you've changed!* Yes, I have. My zip code has changed, my area code has changed, my bank account has changed, my job and career have changed. You are right. I have changed and I'm fine with that. *Oh, you gettin' brand new!* Yes. I like brand new.

Jesus said, "Bring me a donkey so I can ride it into town." As he's on the back of the donkey, everybody's screaming,

"Hosanna, Hosanna! Glory to the King of the Most High!" Right? Wrong. He said, "Bring me a donkey no one's ever ridden" (Mark 11:2). I don't know where people get their doctrine from when it comes to their success and God's desire towards them. People think God glorifies in them being poor, struggling, hurting, sick, and in bad relationships. Why didn't Jesus say, *"I want you to go down to the local swap mart, get me a used donkey, the cheapest one you can find"*? Is it not possible that there are certain areas in our lives where we refuse to walk in light? Because we won't walk in light, God can't move in it. It's not Him coming down to you; it's you deciding to walk in light and realizing that light is progressive. You don't qualify for more light if you refuse to walk in the light that you have.

"Well, I just don't understand, Pastor. I want to understand more and learn more." Are you walking in the light you have? If you're not, stop asking for God to give you more light. You have not mastered what you currently have. Now you become like the parable of the talents where you want ten talents, but you're the one who will bury it in the ground and not use it (see Matthew 25:14). God will not give to you what you will not use. As His Word goes forth, it shall not return to Him void. If He gave it to you and you bury it, you have now caused what He said to be void.

If you want to be a container of the power and the glory of God, then you have to learn how to walk in what you know. If you see it clearly, walk in it! If you understand it, walk in it! If you are weak in a certain area, get understanding and study! Put your head on straight, and get your mind right. Let your soul prosper, and as your soul prospers, so will everything else.

I cannot stand carnal Christians. *I can sleep around a little bit, it's okay. I can go outside of my marriage.* No, you can't.

Nobody talks about sin anymore; they're afraid it will clear their churches. I'm not going to switch up what God tells us to do. There's a point where you have to understand that if you believe you're going to be used in this last day, you will need to step even further into the light. Darkness is pervading this world. If you don't know it, turn on the TV and see what's going on out there. Mothers are killing their own kids! What kind of world do we live in? You don't have to teach people to be evil; they've got that mastered.

My heart goes out to young people because they have to face things I didn't have to face. When we were younger, we'd fight. Whoever got whooped, you got up, the next week you were friends, and you might have been as thick as thieves. Nowadays, they fight, they shoot, they die, and it's eternal over nothing. Some of you are praying for world peace. Knock that off. The Bible never says we're going to have world peace. As a matter of fact, if you've read your Bible, you'll know the times we're in now is a sign of the end times. This was always going to happen. *"God works in mysterious ways. He'll come like a thief in the night!"* Not for you. He'll come like a thief in the night for those who don't know Him. If you know Him, you are in the light. You will not be surprised or shocked at what God is doing. You will not be shocked that the world is where it is today. *"I just wish the world would change."* I don't, because the worse it gets, the uglier it gets, the closer we get to that moment where we look up, the clouds part, and He shall rise up with a roar of a lion! You're afraid because you're not ready. I'm ready! I do rapture practice every once in a while just to see if I can jump.

I understand that we are not going to be shocked. None of this stuff surprises me. This is the way it's supposed to be, but if you want to be used in this time you can't be lukewarm. In Revelation, Jesus says, "I rather you be hot. I rather you be cold.

But what I can't stand is a lukewarm Christian" (Revelation 3:15-16).

You know what lukewarm is? You're not on fire and you're not cold. Some people think that means He'd rather you not be for Him or be on fire for Him. That's not true. In those times, they used tepid water to induce vomiting. That's why He said, "I will spew thee out of my mouth." If you're lukewarm, you're tepid. Tepid is a mixture of hot and cold, neither hot nor cold; it's in the middle. For example, you're a Christian, but you live a sinful life; you can't control your lusts, you hurt people all of the time, you have issues with money. You never support, you never give, you never serve; you just won't give of yourself to God. You're tepid; you're lukewarm.

Years ago, my ex-wife and I had a fish named Oscar. Oscar was a beta fish. One day we went out of town. We couldn't leave Oscar, so we took him with us. When we got back home, my ex-wife grabbed the bowl, placed it under the faucet (it's June in Arizona, mind you), and turned it on. Then she dumped Oscar in it. Now, Oscar's dead. Most people who live in Arizona know that when you turn on the water and it's 115 degrees outside, that water is going to be hot. Let's just say that we put a glass under that same faucet and we turn it on. If you've been sitting outside for two to three hours and I hand you that glass of water, you're going to spit it back out because you want cold water.

When Jesus said hot or cold, He wasn't talking about being for God or not being for God, He was talking about being refreshing. When you are hot, you want something cold. When you are cold, you want something hot. Therefore, in the wintertime, if you grew up in the Northeast like I did and it's 5,000 below zero, believe me when I tell you in 18 inches of snow, there is nothing better than a nice hot bowl of soup. When I'm cold, hot soup is refreshing. There is also nothing worse than a cold cup of coffee. The reason Jesus wants you to be hot or cold is because He wants you to be all the way. Not walking in darkness and then trying to claim light, but you have to be all the way in. He wants you to be refreshing, and what refreshes Him is all of you. It doesn't refresh Him when He has parts of you, because He doesn't want parts of you. He wants all of you.

When you start to give God all of you, when you say, "God, You can have first place in my finances, my relationships, and I'll serve You," all of a sudden, everybody around you throws out the c-word. *"You're in a cult! You're changing!"* So, you'd rather I pay a psychiatrist $150 an hour, experience no change, and still stay enabled and stuck to your co-dependent self? Once I get free, I start walking in victory and God moves; He blesses me and things start to change. My house increases, my life increases, and all these things start changing. Now they have a problem because they're afraid I'm about to leave them behind. Here's the real thing: All you have to do is walk up to them and say, "Won't you come with me?" God is no respecter of persons. If He did it for me, He'll do it for you.

"Well, I'm not ready to walk in that kind of light." I remember Pastor Ricky, my spiritual father, would tell a story about a guy who walked up to him and said, "Sir, that's some of the best preaching I've ever heard in my life." Pastor Ricky said, "Oh, great! So we'll see you tomorrow!" He said, "No." Pastor Ricky responded, "What do you mean 'no'? You said that's some of the best preaching you've ever heard!" He said, "Sir, you're bringing too much light and I just can't handle it."

UNDERSTANDING LIGHT

What do you do with that? Where do you file that? How many times has somebody walked up to you and said, "You're bringing too much light in my life. I won't be back." If you wonder why chickens continue to gravitate toward you...

Pastor Ricky didn't tell the guy to leave. The guy said, "I'm leaving because you're bringing too much light." If you're bringing a lot of light, chickens will be repelled before you say a word. It'll be the anointing that is shut up in your bones that'll agitate them to the place where they'll say, *"Look, I am out of here! I can't put up with you, not another minute."* That's when you say, "Peace, love you! Have a nice life." If I walk in the light as He is in the light, then I have fellowship not only with Him, but with everyone else who is in the light. The only way I can do darkness is I have to shut off the light.

Kenneth Hagin Sr. used to say, "It's dangerous to come up to light and then walk away from it." You would have to turn off the light; you would have to shut off God. You have to be careful of people who know better, but won't do better, and can shut God off to go creep in the dark. They come in the church and as soon as they hit the door, they turn the light on. *I'm holy!* As soon as they get outside, they shut the light off again. You have to be careful of a person who thinks like that. It's interesting how the Bible reveals that God is obligated to destroy all idols, even if you've made yourself one. If you teach me something and it's biblical, I might have to chew on it awhile, but I'll have to take it. If I know it, you've told me, I get it, I see it, it's in the Bible, I understand it. It's doctrine; I can't spit it back out. Sometimes, I'm throwing this stuff at you and you're thinking, *Oh, that's not for me. That's for somebody else.* No it's not. That's for you.

How do you know when people are struggling? Their joy isn't full. They look like they've been on lemon patrol, as if they're sucking on lemons, mad at everybody. They're scowled up and angry. How do you know your joy isn't full? If your joy is full, your joy is full! One of the reasons we don't fill a cup of water to the top is because it'd be too full to drink from. It would spill and water would be everywhere. If your joy is full, your joy will be everywhere. It will spill.

If life is getting the better of you, you have to ask yourself if you're walking in the light. If you're walking in the light, then help is on the way. If you are walking in darkness, don't take this whooping personally. It's nothing I can pray you out of. *"Pastor, please lay hands on me."* I could rub your head until your hair comes off. If you are going to act like the devil, you're going to get what the devil has. If you want to live with the devil, you're going to have what the devil has for you. That's the way it works. There is no way to get around that. However, if you will walk in the light as He is in the light, you will have fellowship with Him and with everyone else. When that happens, now you have intimacy with God. That's when He says He'll protect you, be your shield, your comforter, your stand-by, your helper, strong tower, healer, and your rock. He will hide you when you need to be hidden. He will take care of you. He is Jehovah Jireh, your provider. He is El Shaddai, more than enough. He is all that you need. He places you under his wings and says, *I've got you. I know Satan was after you, but I'm glad you made that decision and stepped on in.* Now, Satan's over there by himself in the dark.

Pastor Nancy Dufresne, Dr. Dufresne's wife, was in a hotel room getting ready for a meeting. Out of the corner of her eye, she saw something sitting in the corner. When she looked over, it was like a little nymph. She saw it and at first she wondered, *What in the world is that*? Now a normal human being would question your own sanity when you see something like that. She started praying in tongues, and when she started praying, God began to give her an interpretation of what she was praying. She was wondering why the being just crouched, sitting there looking at her. God said, *He's just waiting for you to slip up, and the moment you do he's going to jump.* So she prayed in tongues, she commanded it to leave, and it left. It had to because it submitted to the authority Jesus placed on the inside of us. However, think about that for a minute. How many times have we been in a situation in one area of our life and never realized the reason this problem happened over here is because of the stuff we were doing elsewhere? The Bible says give no foothold to Satan. You have to be careful because your footholds will become your strongholds.

When I was in IT sales, we used to sell implementations that would be a million or half a million dollars, three to four million dollar implementations. These were big deals. We would have to get a hold of the C-level of the company. There were times where we couldn't get to them but we knew who they were. I would take an envelope and put a baby shoe in it. Then I would include a letter introducing who we are and who I am, and I would say, *"I just wanted to spend some time and talk with you about how we might be able to help you. P.S., now that I've got a foot in the door, let's talk."*

Psychologically, anything you get in the mail that's lumpy, you'll open. I don't know if you know that or not, but that's why they put those fake cards in the mail. Or they'll put something in it like a pen. You might take the pen out and throw the letter away, but you're going to open it. So here's my point. What I was trying to do was get a foot in the door, because once I get a foot in the door, I had access to the person. I've had people call me back and say, *You know, that's the most original thing I've ever seen. I want to meet with you just because you did that.*

Sometimes Satan sends you little packages. She might be 5'5" with a skirt up to there just because he's trying to get a foot in the door. If you're not careful, your footholds will become your strongholds. So you have to be careful. That's why the Bible says don't give him a foothold (Ephesians 4:27). If he can get his foot in the door, it's on. It's easier to avoid than it is to resist. You have to know he's crouched in the corner waiting. He can't touch you otherwise. He can't do anything to you other than watch. The only thing that allows him to move is you. You have to give him a foothold and once you give it to him, he will wreak havoc.

QUALIFYING FOR MORE LIGHT

"And these things write we unto you that your joy may be full."
—1 John 1:4

When Jesus says "that your joy may be full," that means your joy can be empty. If He's writing to you that your joy may be full, He's saying that you may have the fullness of joy. You can have everything that joy affords you in your walk in life. Joy is absolutely important. The Bible says that the joy of the Lord is our strength (Nehemiah 8:10). It's one thing if every time I have to do anything with you it's a burden to me, but it's another if it's a joy. There's something about having joy and there's something about being in that place that you can be excited and happy about doing whatever it is you have to do.

Jesus is saying, *I'm getting ready to tell you some things that'll fix your life. If you understand this, then your joy will be full.* In other words, you won't have to struggle and you won't have to be in constant sorrow. You won't constantly go from drama to drama and calamity to calamity. He says, "This, then, is the message which we have heard of him, and declare it unto you, that God is light, and in him is no darkness at all" (1 John 1:5). That says a mouthful.

"If we say that we have fellowship with him and walk in darkness, we lie."
—1 John 1:6

Notice he says it's not that we *say* not the truth, it's that we *do* not the truth. People can say a lot of things. I've had people say, "Pastor, I love you. You're my pastor. I'm here for you; we're going to do this thing." But the moment something happens, they're gone; they've left. I wonder, *How it is that I'm your pastor, you tell me you love me, yet you're able to walk out? If I did that to you, you'd have a problem with it. You would question our relationship.* This is why I'm never moved by people who talk about how great things are, especially when it's their first time in the church. People can say a lot of things, but when you watch what they do, it's a manifestation of what they believe; what they say is a manifestation of what they think. There's a difference between what you think and what you believe. You can think a lot of things, but only if you believe it, will it frame and guide your behavior.

If I believe that I'm accountable for the life I have to live, then I deal with things with reverential fear. It's not a fear that I'm going to be hurt, but a reverential fear of disappointing God, knowing that there are things that are pleasing to Him. If we please God by faith, that means God can be pleased. If He can be pleased, then He can also be displeased. I think the hyper-grace nonsense pervading Christianity gives the idea that God doesn't care. That's the message, but how far from the truth is that! That's the problem. There becomes a disconnect between what we do, what we think, what we say, and who we are. How do we build congruency to a place to what we say is what we're thinking, what we're thinking is what we believe, and what we believe is what we do? The Bible says as a man thinketh in his heart, so is he (Proverbs 23:7). If you understand that God has no darkness in Him at all, none, then if you walk in darkness He says you're lying because you do not the truth.

QUALIFYING FOR MORE LIGHT

There's nothing worse than a Christian who says one thing and does something else. When I talk to people who are not involved in church, one of the first things they always say is, "My issue with the church are the hypocrites. People get in church acting one way then go out in the street acting another." My usual response is, "Yes, and there's room for one more." People realize that there is always incongruence. There are always things that will be different than what we expect. If we are to be honest, disappointment in life is when we have a blueprint from our life that didn't happen. It's a lack of congruency to our expectations. When we recognize God's expectations for our life, incongruence for Him is just as disappointing.

He says, "If we walk in the light, as he is in the light, we have fellowship one with another, and the blood of Jesus Christ, his Son, cleanseth us from all sin" (1 John 1:7). What does it take to be cleansed from all sin? We must walk in light. If I am a person who has robbed a bank (I haven't, but for the sake of this discussion let's say I did), if I walk in light and the Bible says Jesus' blood cleanses me of all sin, then the equivalent to that would be as if I'd been absolved of the crime that I committed. However, if I move into darkness, now I have to carry the penalty of whatever happens. If I get caught, then it's a wrap. I now have to deal with the consequence. If you want to get to the place where you are cleansed from sin, or have it removed from you, then you must walk in light. So many people are reaping the penalty of their mistakes because not only were they in darkness, but they refuse to leave darkness. *If I walk in light, you mean to tell me He's able to cleanse me from all unrighteousness? You mean to tell me, no matter what I've done, if I would walk in light...* Yes.

The light is God's Word, the revelation or the revealing of the truth of God's Word. Do you have any idea the things I'll say to people over and over and they just don't get it? They don't get the light. For example, your love walk. There are certain things about your love walk; faith worketh by love. That word "by" is *dia* which means "through." We get the word "diablo" (meaning for the devil) which means to strike repeatedly until you break through. If I understand that faith worketh by love, but yet you can't find it in your heart to love, stop asking why your faith doesn't work. That's light.

Now you can do whatever you want to do. You can get as mad as you want, talk bad about me and everybody around you, but your faith will not work and you will struggle. What you want and think is going to happen is that somehow God will rewrite the rules for you. Now, what *will* happen if you walk in love is that your faith will start to work.

The word "worketh" is *energia* from which we get the word "energy." There are two main words to describe the power of God —*dunamis* and *energia*. "Dunamis" is inherent ability. A stick of dynamite has inherent power. If I set it down, everyone is safe and there's no problem. It can sit the whole time and not cause a problem. Does it have power? Yes, but that power has not been activated. However, if I light that stick, it will clear a building because it will give off energy (or energia), which is dunamis now activated and exploded. So then if faith worketh, or explodes, by love, if your faith is not working for you, you'd better check your love walk. When I say check your love walk, here's what I mean: How do you get along with the people around you; the people you work with, the people at the grocery store? How do you react to someone when you're driving down the street and they cut you off? Are you letting them know they're number one? That's your love walk.

If you can't keep your behavior under control, and you're wondering why your faith is not working, that's light. Light is when the truth of God's Word becomes revealed, as the Bible says in Proverbs 4:18, it shines brighter and brighter unto a perfect day, unto a mature day. If it shines brighter and brighter, then it means revelation, or light, becomes brighter and greater. You can't be in church and act a certain way, then go out in the field with your friends cussing, dropping bombs, and then come back to church and get on the platform. Light brings you to a place where there is no duality. Jesus said what you say must line up with what you do. You're in danger when you act a certain way, live a certain way, yet you know better. It's different when you don't know any better, but when you do know better and you've been taught, you can't go before God and say, "Well, you know what happened was, I didn't know."

I've brought light on some situations for people and they just weren't ready to hear it. When I talk to people about their giving, I'm very selective about whom I discuss it with. However, here's the truth. Your money isn't going to make a difference for me anyway, it makes a difference for you. People think I talk about that a lot. Three quarters of the parables Jesus taught were about money and your possessions because He knew your possessions were something you were supposed to have; they're not supposed to have you. When they have you, you're moved in your giving by your situation. Now if you're moved in your giving by your situation, then if you have, you give, and if you don't, you won't. If the god of this world controls what you can have or don't have, then all he has to do is make sure you don't have, and then you won't. So now he controls you by the pressure of external things. Once Satan realizes that no matter what situation you're in, you're still going to do what God has asked you to do, he figures out a different route of attack because he knows that one doesn't work anymore. The button is disconnected.

When people come to me and tell me what they're struggling with, I ask them about their giving. People will ask, "What does that have to do with my life?" How do you expect God to move in an area in which you refuse to honor Him? That's light. If you want Him to bring you a mate, do you think He's going to bring you one of His children so you can sleep with him/her? You think God's going to sign on to that? Be not deceived, God is not mocked. When you want something, you better ask yourself if you are honoring Him in that area. I've watched people's businesses fail because they won't honor God. I've watched people try to do other things and they just don't work. They stay close enough to want it, but far enough away to never get it because they won't honor God. Then they wonder and they're praying.

Do you ever notice some people's Facebook accounts? It just floors me. They're dropping F-bombs on one post and the next post talking about how good God is. The Bible says, "Let no corrupt [or evil] communication proceed out of your mouth" (Ephesians 4:29). That includes Fleshbook. How can you say one minute, "F so-and-so!" and the next minute talk about God? What light do you have?

If you can't walk in the light you already have, you don't qualify for more light. Kenneth Hagin Sr.'s wife was upset because one lady had a mink coat. She said, "All I have is one dress. I've been traveling with you, we've been faithful to the ministry, and all I have is one dress and that lady's got a mink coat." She wasn't coveting what the lady had, she was disappointed in what she had. He said to her, "Honey, if you stick with me, I'm learning how to hear from the Holy Ghost. If you stick with me, we'll get there."

He was saying he was learning how to increase in light, because when he increased in light, he increased in all areas of his life. With more light comes more responsibility. With more responsibility comes more revelation. With more revelation comes more provision.

If you have places to go in God, you must understand that you have to move into greater degrees of light. If you want to stay back, you'll be fighting on level one, not realizing you're fighting level ten enemies. You cannot stay where you are and think God's okay with that. He loves you too much to leave you there. It's constant and never-ending improvement. It's a constant place of pulling you up because the greater degree of light, the greater degree of provision that comes with it.

So here's what happened: When Kenneth Hagin Sr. died, his wife had a mink coat for every day of the week. They had their own private jet. They got there, but it took them awhile. We want it all and we want it now, especially young people. They want everything and they want it immediately. They don't want to work hard for it, they want an entitlement. *"I think I'm just entitled to this."* You're not entitled to anything if you haven't paid the bills, plain and simple. You have to pay the cost to be the boss. This is the problem for people who want to be in charge, they want to have influence.

It's amazing how many people want to get next to me because they want to whisper in my ear. I don't need you whispering in my ear, my wife does that. It's about paying the cost. *"You want me to serve where? I'm above that!"* That's why you have to start there, and if you tell me that's beneath you, I'm going to go lower. You don't want to sweep the floor? Go clean the toilet. *"Well, that's worse!"* I know. We're going to beat that out of you because light will bring you to a greater place. Light will say, "You know what? I'll do whatever I've got to do. If God is in charge and He tells me to do it, I'll do it." See, I can earn my way to where I need to be. It's so funny how kids will say, *"Well, you don't trust me."* You haven't earned it. Your behavior will tell me whether I can trust you or not. If you're not making good decisions, then I don't trust you. *"Well, you should."* No, I shouldn't.

This is the way things work. People don't understand that light is progressive. That's why it says it gets brighter and brighter unto the mature, perfect day. It comes and takes you to another level. Kenneth Hagin Sr. said, "Baby, if you stick with me...I'm still learning." In other words, he said, "I'm going to make mistakes, but I'm going to get this right and as I get it right, as I grow to the next level, things will start to change and provision will come because I'm walking in greater degrees of light. My relationships will change and my life will change. My provision will change because I'm willing to go to the next step. I'm not sitting here holding on to last year's revelation as if this is what's going to sustain me."

When you are in the fight for your life, sometimes you have to realize that what you had yesterday is not good enough for today. The sandwich you ate last week is no good for today. You need something every single day to take you to the next level. I'm not talking about this wimpy Christianity. That may have worked for your parents, but it isn't going to work for you. I'm talking about people who are fighting for their life every single day and they need something more. *"Well, I don't understand why I just can't move forward."* You won't because you're stuck. You're stuck with your own stinkin' thinkin'. *"Well, God knows my heart."* That's why you should be afraid.

QUALIFYING FOR MORE LIGHT

The truth of the matter is that people don't even know their own hearts, but God does. That's why the Bible says the Word is a two-edged sword that divides the bone and the sinew and it brings you to a place where God is the discerner of the heart and the intentions of man (Hebrews 4:12). He separates inside of you what your real intentions are. If you can't be told what to do, and you think you're just entrepreneurial or you're just a leader, how stupid is that? You can't lead if you don't know how to follow. Everybody knows that, but in their heads they're like, *Well, you know if I was just given an opportunity, I could do it.* You have been given opportunity. You lead every time you sweep a floor. Everything I do, I'm leading. I know eyes are watching. The highest level of leadership is not when people are following you, it's not when you get everybody to think more highly of you, it's when you're able to get everybody to think more highly of themselves. Otherwise you're managing. A manager and a leader are not the same. This is what we struggle with in today's society. We don't have leaders anymore; we have people who want to be paycheck takers, not difference makers. We need difference makers, people who understand they are here to make a difference.

John says if we walk in the light, then the blood of Jesus cleanses us from all sin (1 John 1:7). In other words, it brings us to a place of removing all that is not Him in us. How do I know if you're walking in light or not? By your behavior. The closer you get to light, the more things you do will bother you. If you're not married to him, but you can date him and sleep with him, and it doesn't bother you, you are walking in darkness and the truth is not in you. It should convict you. When you're creeping in that hotel room, what if you heard a knock at the door and it was Jesus? If it doesn't convict you, if you don't feel anything about it, the Bible says you've seared your conscience (1 Timothy 4:2). I call this spiritual vampirism: People show up, they take from the church, they receive word from the church, their life grows, but they don't want to give anything back. It's absolute darkness. How dark do you have to be to think that way?

You go to a move theater and if you go to the little matinee showing before noon you get in for six dollars. Then you get to the concession counter. Last time we were there it cost me forty dollars at the concession counter. Then they had the nerve to say we don't get free refills. Here's what I'm telling you: People will do something that doesn't have any spiritual significance in their life, yet they'll spend all kinds of money. They come to the church and put a dollar in the collection plate. If that's all you can do, then that's all you can do. I'm not talking about the amount, I'm talking about the heart behind it.

I remember the story of a little boy who went to church with his father and they were going to the movies afterwards. When the plate came around at church, the father put a dollar in the collection plate. As he was leaving, they got in the car with the little boy in the back. The father's driving and he's just eating their lunch. *"I can't believe the pastor's sermon... this was a mess! He talked about... and this is just not good... the people there weren't very nice..."* He just ate the lunch of the church. After he got done, the little boy said, "I thought that was pretty good for a dollar."

It's interesting how people think. Again, what you expect and what you get is based on the measure of what you give. This is why one person can walk away from a message and say, *"Wow, that was the best message I've ever heard!"* Yet another person walks away grumbling and upset. I'm going to be honest with you. If you won't learn how to control yourself, you will never walk in victory. *"Well, I just got to keep it real."* Keep it real dumb. This is light. When I taught my message on "Causes," we talked about the reasons people struggle, and we lost one third of the church. People don't want to hear it.

Remember all light is of the same kind, it's just different degrees. What is lawful to do is not always profitable to do. When you've been in the dark for a long time and I hit the lights, or you first wake up and the sun's coming through the window, you're like, *"Good God, really?"* Let's take music for example. If I want to implant suggestions in your head, then all I have to do is set it to music. That's why the Bible says that we are lively stones (1 Peter 2:5) and we sing unto ourselves in psalms, hymns, and spiritual songs (Ephesians 5:19). If you have any spirituality in you, hearing certain things should rub you wrong. It should hit your spirit.

You might be at a place where you're just getting into this thing and there's grace for that. However, if you've been around long enough, there's a point where you should know better. If you've been in church for 30 years and you're still rocking 2Pac every time you leave, you have a problem. You haven't grown up. *"Well, I just love all types of music."* Okay, but here's the problem. I remember Pastor Nancy, the late Dr. Dufresne's wife, was going to buy her son a drum set. She talked to her brother who was a musician. He told her to buy him a good drum set because otherwise, if he learned on a poor quality drum set, it would ruin his ear. He'll learn sound based on the wrong things. Then when he gets in the right place, he will not be able to perform correctly because he will have learned through his ears incorrectly. You have to guard what goes into your ears and your eyes and you have to be at a place where you understand the necessity of that based on walking in light.

I know I'm hitting people in certain areas where they don't want to grow, but you cannot tell me why you are rolling down the street, busting your eardrums to stuff that is absolutely not glorifying—not only to God, but to women and men and people in general. You cannot tell me that God is in the car with you, sitting there like, "Yeah, this is my jam right here!" You cannot tell me that the Holy Spirit on the inside of you is saying, "Yeah! This is what we listen to in heaven! Jesus is rockin' this in His Bentley, this is it! This is the hotness!" That doesn't make any sense. If you have the Holy Ghost on the inside of you, do you have the understanding that He goes wherever you go? If He goes wherever you go, do you know that you can grieve Him? And if you can grieve Him, then what do you think the outcome of that is? If the Bible says that your body is the temple of God (1 Corinthians 6:19), that when He rent the temple and He no longer lives in a temple made with hands and you have become the temple, then what you do in your body you are doing to His temple.

How do you know you have a call of God on your life? *I believe that somewhere along the line I am supposed to do something great for God!* If you have a call of God on your life, here is what you are supposed to do. You are supposed to find somebody who's already walking in a call and submit yourself to it. Their responsibility, should they choose to accept it, is to then develop you into whatever it is you are called to be. Even if they're a pastor and you're called to be a prophet, it doesn't matter because they're walking in the ministry, and they can develop anything. However, you'd better find that right person, because if you don't, you can put yourself in a place of danger.

Jonah was called to go to Nineveh (Jonah 1:2). God said, "I want you to go there and tell them they're not behaving correctly and if they don't get it together, then I'm going to release judgment on them." So Jonah says, "I ain't going to do it!" He goes the opposite direction and boards a boat with a bunch of other people.

All of a sudden, judgment comes on the boat. Did God so graciously pull everybody off the boat, except for Jonah, because they were innocent? No, everybody on the boat with Jonah was now reaping what Jonah had sown. God sent Jonah to deliver Nineveh from the judgment, but the same judgment God was not willing to pour on the people was now on Jonah and everyone in the boat.

Some people can say no. They will live moderately successful lives. They will die, they'll still make it to heaven. They won't have anything up there, but they'll make it. For most, they'd rather sleep on the streets of gold. It becomes clear that Jonah is the reason why this is all happening. So everybody on the boat said to Jonah *"You have to go. We don't know you, we ain't fitting to die for you, and we're not going back to port because we might not make it. You have to go right now."*

Why would God pour judgment out on Jonah and not on the people? Jonah was called. I've watched people die because they were unskilled with the anointing and the call that was on their life. I've watched people become sick, get close to death, and lose everything in their life. I've watched so many things happen to people who refused to walk in what God had for them and to submit themselves to the process that He had for them. They knew they were called. *"Maybe next year when my job lets up. Maybe when this changes, maybe when this happens..."* They have a laundry list of excuses.

Kathryn Kuhlman said she told God when He first revealed to her what He wanted her to do, "God, I'm not capable. Surely there's a man who can do this." God told her, "I asked a couple men to do it and they wouldn't do it. Now I'm telling you." It's recorded historically that this is a woman who walked in such a great degree of anointing that they had to shut down the Pittsburgh airport. As she walked through, they thought somebody had released a bomb or chemical agent because people were falling out under the power of God by the droves in the airport. I'm talking about an anointing; the power of God when you can go and sit next to somebody and all of a sudden the anointing on your life moves them to a place where they just want to tell you everything they've been through and repent to you. You'll say, *It's not me, it's Him!* What happened to the real power of God? Why is the church being so outmaneuvered? People won't walk in light. They're not coming up to light. They're expecting light to come down to them.

They had to put in a special entrance to usher Kathryn Kuhlman underground and up to the plane because she couldn't go through the airport. Here she is on national television, one of the first to ever do it that way, one of the first to have her own private jet. All of these things that God blessed her with could have been for somebody else but they refused to do it because they were not paying attention. How many people will die with the anointing inside of them as opposed to making a difference in this world? How many people will walk completely out of the power of God in their life just because they want to be stubborn, hard-headed, and stupid? Seriously? We have a call. There's a purpose to our lives. I was not born just to sit around and do nothing. I was made for this!

Here's the reality of it. If I'm ever going to walk in it, I have to walk in light. My light is different than yours—the same light, but a different degree. If your degree is at a certain place, then walk in it. Stop giving yourself excuses. Stop making it easy for you to not hear what's being said. It's so funny how I'll bring correction and the first thing people want to do is tell me excuses. I'm like, "Seriously? Here's the world's smallest violin. I'll play it for you." I don't want to hear none of that, I don't care. When we're going to war, I don't care. What person goes to war and doesn't count the cost? We are in the middle of a battle. We are fighting for people's lives. We are fighting for their souls; we are at war! Don't try, let's do.

When you walk in light, you qualify for more. This is why Hagin said to his wife if she'd stick with him, they'd get there. He was going to walk in the light he had and that qualified him for more. As he continued on, she may not have had but one dress, but he would line her closet with dresses. She may not have but one mink coat, but he'll line her closet with mink coats. It wasn't about the stuff, because if it was about the stuff, he would have said, "Baby, I'll quit the ministry and get a corporate job. I'll quit coming to church and I'll get another job." What he realized is that there was no way in the world his job could be better to him than God. God said if I would give what I would give to Him to them, then He will bless me for it. There's nothing wrong with me having anything as long as God is my source. If He brought it into my life, then I can have it and no devil in hell can take it from me. That sounds like a good deal to me!

I know many people who have a call of God on their life and they have been neglectful and downright disrespectful towards God concerning that call, then they wonder why they struggle with Him. They wonder why they're struggling in life and why things don't seem to work out well. They wonder why they seem to get so close, but yet so far. It's because they are not dealing with Him according to their light.

> *"And this is the condemnation, that light is come into the world, and men loved darkness rather than light, because their deeds were evil."*
> —John 3:19

How did Jesus know they loved darkness more than they loved the light? If God is light and light has come into the world, then He says they love darkness more than they love God. How did He know? It was because of the things they were capable of doing. He said there's no way if God is working in you that you could do this.

There used to be a thing called "Smash or Pass" on Facebook. Here's what's happening: The self-esteem of our youth is so low that they require everybody else to prop them up. So they put it out, *Do you like me? Do you think I'm cute?* Of course, someone always responds. Smash or Pass means, "Would you have sex with me or would you pass?" First of all, how low is your self-esteem to even put something out there like that, but then post quotes about how great God is? You are prostituting yourself. By your deeds, how much darkness do you walk in? You think it's okay because you're just playing; it's only hypothetical and nothing serious. God said if you even think evil toward your brother, you've murdered them. Whether you like it or not, you know it's truth.

> *"For everyone that doeth evil hateth the light, neither cometh to the light, lest his deeds should be reproved. But he that doeth truth cometh to the light, that his deeds may be made manifest, that they are wrought in God."*
> *—John 3:20-21*

People don't like their stuff being brought to light because they think they can do good, God, and Satan all at the same time. They think if they do enough God, that will wash out evil. I come to light and bring myself to light, so now I've proven what I do is to God. Anything that has to be done in secret and no one can know about can't come to light.

> *"No man, when he hath lighteth a candle, putteth it in a secret place, neither under a bushel, but on a candlestick, that they who come in may see the light. The light of the body is the eye; therefore, when thine eye is single, thy whole body also is full of light; but when thine eye is evil, thy body also is full of darkness. Take heed, therefore, that the light which is in thee be not darkness."*
> *—Luke 11:33-35*

If it's right, nobody hides it. If you have to hide it, you know it's wrong even if you've justified it within yourself to do it. *You mean to tell me that I might not be able to tell that light is really not light?* Jesus said be careful not to allow the light that's in your eyes be darkness. He says if your whole body be full of light, having no part dark, then the whole shall be full of light and the bright shining of a candle will give you light. It's so interesting how He says if your eye is focused, then your body cannot have darkness in it. It's when the duality comes in where I am one thing but I act another. Now I'm not focused on one light, I am focused on multiple things. Now light is entering into my body, but at the same time, so is darkness. He said be careful because you can think it's light and be walking in darkness.

I got a phone call the other day from somebody who started out: *I'm having a problem and I need to meet with you.* I don't even know him. I never met him before in my life, but he wanted to meet with me. I said, "Well, that's great. So what's your problem?" He said, "I'd rather talk to you in person." "No, you're going to tell me what you want first because I don't have time for that. I don't even know you." "Well, you see, I'm on this special mission. I don't have to go to church. I've got this special relationship with God and God has revealed some things to me that I need to have somebody talk to me about." So I said, "What church do you go to?" "I don't go to church; I don't have to." "Okay. All right. So, you don't have to go to church?" "No." I said, "You know that's unscriptural, don't you?" "Well, see, you know, the type of ministry that I have…"

The whole time I'm thinking, *Dear God, if I had have taken this meeting…sitting in my office listening to this, I would have ripped his arms off and beat him with them. I ain't been saved that long and I'm not that sanctified! Thank you, God, for not letting me get in this position.* So I said, "You know that's unscriptural, right? Everything you just said is unscriptural." "Well, no pastor has even been able to prove it to me." "Well okay, let's talk about Hebrews 10:28. Let's talk about how it was Jesus' habit to go to church." I just broke it down. He said, "Well, I just have this special thing, I just need to sit down with you." I said, "Here's what I'm going to tell you to do. Find yourself somebody, a church you can submit to, and then submit."

He was full of light but it wasn't the same kind. That's why I keep saying to you that all God light is of the same kind, it's just varying degrees. Remember, the Bible calls Satan a light bearer (2 Corinthians 11:14). You can have light and think you have it clear, but you had better be careful. Is it you, or is it God? Do you have support, or do you not?

The caller then started talking about the book of Enoch, the Apocrypha, and all of this other stuff. I said, "Here's the problem. The Canon of Scripture does not mean that's the only thing out there; it means this is the only thing we have that agrees. The Bible is canon. 'Canon' means that these are the books that have been put together that all agree. In other words, there's no discrepancy between them. It does not mean that this is the totality of all that God is. It means this is all *we* have. It's all the light we have. That's why the Bible says in Deuteronomy 29:29 that the secret things belong to the Lord.

"So if you want to get into a debate over who Cain's wife was, I'm not going to argue about it with you and I'm not going to preach doctrine because I don't know. It does not say. The light that we have does not explain it. Therefore, I'm only able to walk in the light that I have. If God said the secret things belong to Him, then that means the only light that I can walk in is the light I was given. The only measure that I'm supposed to measure myself against is the light that I have been given. However, if I don't even know the light that I have, then I can walk in a different type of light and think that I have some higher calling than everybody else does."

I told him to go find somebody else to talk to. He said, "I've been thrown out of churches."

I could see why. I wasn't going to throw him out of mine, I wouldn't even let him in in the first place. I'm supposed to take oversight thereof and protect this organization from the wolves. I don't mind if you're a goat; you can be stubborn. The Bible says God will deal with the stubborn ones. That's not my job. It's my job to teach. God will deal with them, but the wolves I will not allow. I've preached many a wolf out the door because when I start bringing light, wolves get upset, offended, and start murmuring to people. *"You heard that message Pastor said? He just ain't right."* Do you have some scripture to prove that? *"Well no, but I know it in my spirit!"* We're expected to walk in the light and it's not all light; it's God's light. That's why the Bible says, "How great does darkness have to be to overcome light?" (Matthew 6:23).

COMING UP TO LIGHT

This is what happens when you're a Christian in darkness. Even though your light is bright, it's still not His light. You can bring some illumination because if you're in a pitch-black room, it would be bright. In the darkest of darkness, light shines, but we can't keep it light, because darkness is the absence of light. Darkness is dependent upon light. Darkness can't make itself, so how great does the darkness have to be to overcome the light in you? How powerful do darkness, lies, and evil have to be to overcome the light that's in you? Light is not dependent upon darkness; darkness depends on light.

APPLICATION OF LIGHT

"If we say that we have fellowship with him, and walk in darkness, we lie, and do not the truth."
—1 John 1:6

We have a challenge, particularly with young people. Usually as you get older, you realize how little you truly know, but young people seem to have a thing in their head that says, *I've got all the answers.* The problem is they do have all the answers, it's just to the wrong questions. Walking in light is in the way you become mature and understand that there's a certain way to do things. If there's a certain way God wants this thing done, then we need to modify our behavior to line up with what we know. When we do that, we walk in light. Sometimes people think, *If I understand what God wants, then I'm in the light.* You're not in light just by hearing and understanding what God wants. The Bible says, "Faith comes by hearing, and hearing by the word of God" (Romans 10:17). Faith does not come by what you heard; faith comes by what you're hearing, but understanding what you're hearing still does not *release* faith. You have to receive what is coming to you so you can take it and do something with it. The moment you do something with it, that now qualifies as faith. You can no more walk in light just because you know what the Bible says than you can be in a marital relationship with someone just because you know them. Do they know that?

People take their knowledge of the Bible and think they have light. You don't have light until you have revelation. The problem is, no one knows when revelation is going to hit. You could hear something ten times and on the tenth time say, "Oh my God, I just got it!" This is where walking in light goes beyond what you say or what you hear. It is a place where it moves beyond your head, beyond your heart; it gets into your feet and you start to do it. You start to walk it out and recognize the things God wants to deal with in you.

The voice of God comes in the voice of your conscience. Do you wonder why people don't have any conscience about the things they do? It surprises me, it really does. Somewhere along the line you'd think that something inside of you said, *I wouldn't do that. Girl, you're going to church. Make sure that dress is a little bit longer. There's no way it should be so tight that you could sit on a piece of bubble gum and tell what flavor it is!* You *know* better, but you don't *do* better. There's a difference between what you know and what you do. You have to ask yourself, Is God pleased with just what I know, or is He pleased with what I do?

That's why He says if we say we have fellowship with Him and we walk in darkness, we lie. If you truly have fellowship with God, you don't do dark things. You guard your mouth. In your language, f-bombs and all kinds of stuff doesn't come out all over the place. *Well,* you say, *I was angry!* You were in the flesh. If we're in the light, do we turn off the lights for a moment so we can act stupid? God has expectations of us to walk in love. You can tell when people are flesh-ruled as they're easily offended; they pick up their marbles and they go home. Childish behavior. When you walk in light, you are doing what God says to do. Now you have taken the Word of God and internalized it to the point where you have measured it against yourself. You say, *"Okay, these are the areas I've got to start walking in. I need to start changing some things because this is ungodly."* You can't be a person who thinks that God is okay with behavior that is inconsistent with His Word. You have deified yourself beyond God and you've rendered His Word of no effect. This is where it gets complicated.

God has a certain way of doing things and it is not our way; it's His way. If His way is higher than our ways, then that means you may not comprehend it. If you cannot comprehend, that's fine, but when you don't comprehend and you still do things His way, that qualifies as faith. People get to a place where they have their little pet sin. *"Oh, God's okay with that. I'm growing. I'm working on it. You know, Pastor, you have to teach more grace."* At what point was grace used as a measure of sin? The Romans asked Paul, "Does this now mean that we can go sin?" He said of course not! (Romans 6:1). This is the place where light becomes real. When it becomes real, we now have to walk in what light we have. When we walk in the light we have, we change.

Walking in light brings freedom. Did you ever notice how Satan likes to use guilt to keep you from coming boldly before the throne? You know how it is: You act up, you do something wrong, Satan will hit you with it. *"You know God won't move for you. Remember last night? Remember this morning? Remember last week?"* Once you have gotten into darkness, Satan has the ability to influence you. That's why Jesus says when you walk in light, then you are cleansed from all sin. Satan has no ability to bring guilt and condemnation against you because you're walking in the light even if you don't completely understand.

People think, *When I get it, I'll do it.* The problem is, as long as it's taking you to get it and do it, Satan is swinging and throwing everything he can. However, the moment you get it and do it, he doesn't have the ability to affect you anymore because now you are walking in the light. In light, there is no darkness. The truth of the matter is none of us can ever be perfect, so we will never be able to completely avoid the attacks of the enemy, but some of us are going through things we don't have to go through. We're going through them because we won't walk in light. We're going through them because the decisions that we've made are affecting not only us but it's affecting our families, our children, our friends, and other people around us.

If you think you are not required to walk in light, it moves beyond just your stubbornness. You're going to take somebody with you. Now you're derailing somebody else. This concept of walking in light is so important because Jesus said once we walk in light, we have fellowship one with another, and the blood of Jesus cleanses us from all sin (1 John 1:7). It renders Satan incapable of railing accusation against us. When he rails accusation against you, it's because of our behavior. That's what gives him his license to behave.

I've seen people struggle with sickness and disease because they would not walk in light. They've heard over and over again, *"You have to love your brothers and your sisters,"* but they refuse to do it and they're as sick as a dog. When Satan brings sickness into your life, the doctors can never figure out what it is. That's a surefire way to know it's an overt attack on your life. It's always a moving target. There are people who are sick because they refuse to tithe. I don't care, keep your money; you're going to need it. It's bizarre that when you have solid spiritual practices, you see greater provision in your life. However, when you don't have spiritual discipline, you find that Satan has the right to do whatever it is that he desires to do. What is it that's going to stop him?

What is sin? Let's break it down in its most basic form. Sin is disobedience to God. When He says, "Let no corrupt communication proceed out of your mouth. I want you to love your neighbor as you love yourself. I want you to be modest," He wants you to do it. These are things God requires of you. When He says you should be going to church, that's His Word and you should be doing it. James says that anything you know to do and you don't do it, that's sin to you (James 4:17). In other words, if you don't know any better, how can you be judged against what you don't know?

This is the whole point of walking in light. It's so difficult to get this point across because there's a stubbornness that has justified itself that it's okay when it's not okay. If we want to live victorious lives, then we have to make a decision in ourselves that we're either going to live this thing for God, or we're not. You can't live like the world and act like the world and then want to praise God. You can't be posting nonsense on one post on your Facebook page and the next post talk about how great God is. You're a hypocrite and light's not in you. If you can go there, then light's not in you. The Bible tells you to avoid even the appearance of evil (1 Thessalonians 5:22). That's a given. Don't even have the appearance of doing it. *"Well, I feel like Christians shouldn't judge."* You know that's an undercover way of keeping your sin your pet, right? The truth of the matter is, if *you* judged it and dealt with it, then nobody else would have an opportunity to judge it.

As Christians, we have a right to judge what we know and believe. I don't know where people get that nonsense from. *"Don't judge me."* Seriously? I won't convict you, I'm not going to sentence you, but anything that you do outside of Christian character or morality, we are going to judge. I am not *of* this world, I am just *in* this world. If I have the Holy Ghost on the inside of me, then I have Holy Ghost discernment. If I have Holy Ghost discernment, then I have the same discernment that you have. Sometimes I wonder if people are genuinely born again because they say that they are, but then they do things of which you know the Holy Ghost does not agree.

Likewise, some people have varying sets of rules. When they come to church, they have a set of rules; when they go home or go to work or school, they have a whole different set of rules. You understand God is everywhere; do you know that? Doctrinally we might not be aware that God is at your job, at your school, in your laptop, or in your phone. If you're walking in light, God expects you to continue to progress. What you used to get away with last year, you are not going to be able to get away with next year. As we grow, we're expected to move into greater degrees of light. The Bible says in Proverbs that light shines brighter and brighter unto the perfect day (4:18). What is the perfect day? It's not perfect as in perfection, but perfect as in mature. Trust me. I have room to grow. There are things I'm still growing in, plenty of things I've done without full revelation, and as I did them, revelation and understanding came.

> *"Daniel answered and said, Blessed be the name of God forever and ever, for wisdom and might are his, And he changeth the times and the seasons; he removeth kings, and setteth up kings; he giveth wisdom unto the wise, and knowledge to those that know understanding; He revealeth the deep and secret things; he knoweth what is in the darkness, and the light dwelleth with him."*
> —Daniel 2:20-22

Have you ever noticed that seasons tend to change—not necessarily by the calendar, they just change? Every March 18th is not the same. It is not governed by the calendar, it's governed by God. If He brings a blizzard in the springtime, He has every right to do that because it is what it is. It's not governed by a clock or a calendar. The Bible says He sets up kings and He tears down kings. In other words, He puts people in office and He takes them out of office. He's the one who brings knowledge, wisdom, and understanding.

People say knowledge is power, but it is not. Knowledge is *potential* power. Wisdom is power because wisdom is the application of knowledge; how you apply what you know. That's why it says He gives wisdom to the wise and knowledge to them that have understanding. Once you have understanding, then you get knowledge. Once you have knowledge, you can now have wisdom of how to apply it. He gives more wisdom to those who learn how to apply, or in other words, do. Then He goes on and says He knows what's in the darkness; you don't. When you won't walk in light, this is why you stumble in the darkness. Once you get over into a place of darkness without light, you can't see. What you can't see is what will hurt you. This is why you need light.

Daniel made it clear. He said, "Look, this is where God works. He works in the light." So any darkness that comes against your life, if you will walk in light, light will immediately illuminate it and give you wisdom as to how to deal with the situation. If I walk in light, then anytime darkness comes against me, as soon as I step in, the fact that I'm walking in light removes darkness and now I can see very clearly. God will give me wisdom how to do this because before I even got there, what was dark before I showed up, God already knew what was there. He says, "Look, go this way and step to this side and you'll miss it completely." He can help me to move away from something before I fall in it.

So many people live in a place where all they think is, *"Let me try this and see if it works."* When they get their butts handed to them, they're thinking, *"Wait a minute, let me try this."* They do a trial-and-error process with God. If I made the decision to walk in true light, then God will navigate my path and anything that is darkness, by the time I get to it, light will be there because if I walk in light, then I understand I am surrounded by light. I am enclosed by light, I am in Christ and Christ is in me.

People tell me, "Pastor, I'm going through this and I'm struggling through that..." You're not walking in light, then you wonder what's your solution. You're in darkness; that's why you don't have the solution. Walking in darkness leaves more questions than answers. God says, "If you understand how to walk in light with Me, then I have the answers because I've searched the darkness. I already know before you get there. What I'm going to do is, because you have understanding, I'm going to give you knowledge. Once I give you knowledge, I'm going to give you the wisdom of how to deal."

This is why I expect favor everywhere I go. I expect that if I walk in light, God's going to show me what to do. He's going to pull me aside and say, "Listen, if you make the wrong decision, here's what's going to happen, but if you do this one, that's the right decision." Now I make my way prosperous—not because I tried one and it failed, but because the spirit of the man is the candle, the light of the Lord searching all the inward parts of the belly (Proverbs 20:27). He's telling you that your human spirit is what He uses like His candle. He takes your spirit and He leads you wherever he wants you to go. Let's put it into today's terms. Your human spirit is His flashlight so that when He takes you through dark places, when you encounter dark places, it might have been dark before you. If I take a candle and it's pitch black in the room, I don't know what's in front of me beyond a certain distance based on the brightness of the candle. Everything within my purview I can see because I have a candle. If God already knows what's in the darkness and by the time I get to it, it is now lit up, then He uses your spirit—not your flesh, your feelings, emotions, your head, or your line of thinking. *"If God was around today and He wrote the Bible today, He wouldn't put some of the things in there that He put in there."* Are you serious? He said, "I charge not." His Word is the same yesterday, today and forever.

Your head doesn't have to know where you're going. You want to know something that happens to me often? I'll be in a place with people where I know things before I even know why I know it. I start talking and saying things to people and sometimes I don't even know why I'm saying what I'm saying. I've slipped over into the place of the spirit where my human spirit now becomes God's candle and He's literally leading me. If I yield my mouth to it, I'll speak things and I will not understand why I'm speaking them because my head is unfruitful, but I'm walking in light. I'm walking in revelation and understanding. All of a sudden I'll start talking and saying things. To the person listening they're like, "Wow, that's it!" For me, I'm thinking about going fishing.

There's a point where you can become so sensitive to the spirit of God that He will literally grab your light and move it by your spirit. He'll take you and navigate you through life's challenges. However, if you're in the flesh, you're literally blowing out the light. Every time you get angry, get into your flesh and start getting offended and hurt and angry, cussing everybody out, you're blowing out the light. Then you wonder why darkness is having its way. If the spirit of man is the candle of the Lord, then it's all about recognizing where He is leading me.

Once I hit my light, I now have a certain purview of what I can see. Even in places where it was dark and you couldn't see, as

51

soon as I bring light, you can. If God knows what's in the darkness, depending on the light that I have, that will determine how much of that light is exposed. The more light I walk in, the brighter it becomes and now I'm able to see further.

The Body of Christ truthfully doesn't understand this teaching. When the Bible says that the light grows brighter and brighter, it's telling you that it gets deeper and wider. As you walk in more light, you see more problems. However, if you're one of those people who refuse to walk in light, you'll stumble. You'll have this little, teeny flashlight trying to figure out what's going on. When you start walking in light, it qualifies you for more light. Next thing you know, you have a huge spotlight. So when I turn on my light, even if it is dark, the whole room gets bright because I'm walking in light. Now when I walk in light I have revelation, understanding, and I can see it coming. All I need is for someone to say something to me and I can tell. Before they even open their mouth, I can tell by the discernment of the Holy Ghost. I can get in the room with them, look at them, and know.

People wonder how they became involved in a relationship with somebody and didn't realize who they were, but they don't have a flashlight. Why do you think they keep the club dark? You think she's Betty Rubble, but you get outside and she looks like Mr. McGillicuddy. How does that happen? You have to recognize that a lot of the things you find yourself in is because you won't walk in light. You're like, *"The devil just tripped me up."* No, he didn't. You tripped yourself up walking around with that little flashlight. The Bible says you have to let your light shine before men (Matthew 5:16). Even little kids know better! This is why you can walk into a place (those of us who walk in light) and people will not like you just because you showed up. They'll start hating on you and you haven't done a thing, but light showed up. The

Bible says that when light showed up, the darkness comprehended it not (John 1:5). The word "comprehended" means we have better understanding because we have a certain level of comprehension. To comprehend something means to get your mind around it; you figure it out. Darkness could not comprehend the light, or let me say it a better way, darkness could not *apprehend* light. When real light shows up, darkness cannot apprehend it.

When you walk in light, Satan cannot stop you. If you want to know the answer, walk in light. Once you bring light into a dark situation, Satan cannot apprehend you. He cannot stop you because he cannot get his mind around it. He cannot figure it out. He's left in darkness and dumbfounded. Every dark situation you walk into, light should have gone before you. It might have been dark before you got there, but once you showed up, help just showed up. I'm serious. If God is in you, then once you show up, light should have just showed up. Understanding should be in you. When understanding is in you, then knowledge comes. When knowledge comes, then wisdom comes with it so you know how to apply it. Now I may walk into a situation and I don't have any answers, but I can pray about it. I can pray in the Holy Ghost, I can pray in tongues, and all of a sudden answers come. Sometimes people are like, *"How did you know how to solve that problem? You must have faced that before."* I didn't. I've never seen that problem before. How did I figure it out? By the Holy Ghost. Because when light shows up, answers come.

This is why people struggle because they think that everything is natural. If God is the revealer of mysteries and He resides on the inside of you, and He says that your spirit is now His candle, when God directs you, do you have any idea the things that He will guide you into? The opportunities that He will lead you to? The people He will put in your path?

You're working overtime trying to make a little bit, and God's saying, "If you would just become sensitive to me..." I remember one time I was ministering and God told me to do something with a person who was leading praise and worship at the time. I had him stand in front of me and I put my hand on his chest. I swayed and at first he just stood there. I began to tap as I swayed and I said, "God's teaching you to flow with Him." Before long, he was right in sync with me. As we swayed back and forth, God was downloading into him how to be led by Him.

God's not going to push you, pull you, or smack you, He's going to lead you by the candle. As He grabs a hold of your human spirit and takes you places, and by your flesh you go the wrong way, He's saying, "We're going that way." He doesn't yell at you; it's that still small voice. How do you learn to be influenced by the subtleties of his presence? Walking in light. This is why what you do is so important. The Bible says all have sinned and fallen short of the glory of God (Romans 3:23). If all have sinned and fallen short of the glory of God, when I think about this, I process it and say, "Let's make sure we understand something."

All have sinned. That's the first thing He's telling me. Therefore, I will never be able to not sin. If anybody says they don't sin, they're a liar. Then I have to think, "What Satan tells me is if I sin, then God doesn't love me anymore because I'm a sinner." We have to get past that because we know Jesus died on the cross for us so that we would not die unto sin. If He died 2,000 years ago and all sin was placed upon His back and with every lash and every beating, every drip of His blood, every tear of His skin, He became unrecognizable for the sins of the world, then I have to know that doctrinally the penalty has now been paid for sin. So if nothing will ever separate me from the love of God and the Bible says that no one can ever snatch me out of His hand if I am His child (John 10:28), then I know I have eternal security as long as I believe and have not renounced my belief. That means that if I'm saved, I'm saved.

If all have sinned and fallen short of the glory of God, then the glory of God is actually the power of God—not the love of God, not even the salvation of God, it's the power. If I am disobedient—and I understand that as I become more Christian, I become less carnal. Paul said, "There are things I'd like to share with you but I can't tell you because you're too carnal. I can't tell you certain things that I'd love to share with you that God has shared with me personally." God took Paul up to the throne and deposited things in him, then he put him back on earth to do a job. Can you imagine this man saying, "I can't even tell you what I would love to tell you because your bulb is too dim." Now he dies with all of it inside because they wouldn't walk in light.

All have sinned and fallen short. To fall short means there's a measure by which I am supposed to obtain, a place where God wants me to be. There is actually a redemptive plan for your life God has that is above where you are right now. Because you are stuck struggling in the nonsense of the day-to-day, you are missing the idea that wherever you are right now, God's plan for you is much higher. Falling short means I'm not hitting the mark, no matter who I am. Here's the problem: We get into services, we hear stuff, and we say, *"Oh, that wasn't for me. Pastor's talking about that, it's not for me."* No, it is for you because all have sinned and fallen short. You have never arrived. If you think you've arrived, then you've missed it because all have sinned and fallen short of the glory of God, which is the power of God.

If I am propagating a grace message that says you can still sin and be okay with God, am I right? Yes I am. I am absolutely correct if I tell you that through grace you are still okay with God. If you sin, make mistakes, mess up, God still loves you. You are still saved. All have sinned and fallen short of the glory of God, the power of God. What I cannot tell you is that you will still walk in the same power. So, if I cannot keep you from getting saved, then what I can do is keep you powerless and render you of no effect. How do I do this? What I do is, I get preachers to start preaching this grace message. It's not that you lose your salvation; you are still saved. As long as you are here on this planet, you will not walk in the power that God has for you. All have sinned and fallen short. That means that when you face challenges and trials in your life, you say, *"I fell into this temptation, I fell into this problem,"* you aren't walking in light. If you are walking in light, the light would have come that was necessary to overcome and to get victory and the power would have been there.

The reason Christians feel so powerless in a world that is kicking their tails is because they do not understand that if you don't walk in light, you have nothing. There will be no power, your prayers will fall to the ground like lead balloons. I need my prayers to work. When I confess something, I need it to happen. I'm not begging for it, I'm commanding, I'm making a decree. This is the way it's supposed to be. Devil, you will not have my life! Devil, you will not have my children! Devil, you will not function in my life! Why? Because I am walking in light.

The more light I walk in, the greater the measure of power. No matter how great, it's still short. If I have a bar and God has a certain level He wants me to walk in, then it's hard for me to blame God when I'm not walking in it. The psychology is, "Maybe God wants me to struggle." But if I've fallen short, that reveals that what He wanted may not be happening in my life, but it does not change the fact that He wanted better. If I'm not walking in better, whose fault is that? This is where people have mixed this grace thing. I call it greezy grace. It's so watered down because it almost tells you can do whatever you want to do because God still loves you. It's a truth wrapped in a lie. God does love you no matter what. No matter how much of an egghead you are, He loves you. No matter how meaty and carnal you are.

Paul was writing to the church, to saved people, when he said, "You're too carnal." He was basically saying, "Even though you are saved, you act like the world acts." You understand your mind, will, and emotions are not saved. I know we say saving souls, but we are not actually saving their soul. Their spirit is what was born again. Which, by the process of their spirit being born again, their soul is saved but it is not reborn. You are going to have to tear down your soul and build it back up. This is why you don't need chicken soup for your soul. What you need is to tear it down and build it back up. In your soul is that place of your emotions, your fears, where you make decisions against God. When you know what God says and you do the opposite, to you it's sin. If it's sin to you and all have sinned and fallen short of the glory of God, then you understand it's sin that causes you to fall short of His power. It is not short of His love or salvation, it's short in His power. When you don't see His provision in your life, when you pray and you feel like nothing is happening, have you recognized that it's a lack of walking in light?

If the Body of Christ would get a hold of this, it would throw those grace teachers. What they're doing is, they're not teaching heresy per se, but they're stripping the church of its power. As they're stripping the church of its power, then there are other agendas that seem to have crept into the world. As those agendas have crept into the world, the church has had no power to stand up against it and say, "No, we're not going to let that happen. You're not going to redefine marriage. You're not going to take this out of school. You're not going to change the Pledge of Allegiance." Have you noticed that over the last years, a decade or two, things have completely changed. If you actually catch it, you will notice that this whole grace thing started about the same time. It's not new, by the way. This whole grace thing was back in the days of Martin Luther, and it's resurfacing.

Walking in light is everything, even when you don't agree or understand. As you walk in light, you qualify for more. As you qualify for more light, you have greater power at your disposal. That's why the higher you go, the more consecrated your life has to be. You can't be an elder or a deacon in the church and act like somebody who just arrived. The same power that should be coursing through you, the same light that was meant to help you, will now be there picking you apart because the expectation is different. That's why the Bible says be careful what you teach. It warns who teach to be careful because they'll be held to a higher standard (James 3:1-2).

I don't take it lightly when I see these guys going in on this greezy-grace message. They're not taking people into hell, they're stripping the church of its power. When we pray, our prayers are hitting like lead balloons and we're wondering why the church has no power. What happened to the days where the Quakers prayed so hard and led such consecrated lives. The reason they called them Quakers is because they started to shake. What happened in the days of Evan Roberts where he preached a message and the power of God fell? People were riding along in their horse and buggy, pulling over and running into the church to repent because the power of God was so strong, and the light was so great. It's a consecrated life.

If you're not circumspect about your behavior, if you don't think about the things you do, YOLO (you only live once), it's dumb. Satan wants you to live. He wants you to be born, live, and die useless. We're playing right into that when we don't understand light. We're not clear about what light is, what our responsibility is. If you have understanding greater than other people about things, that's a responsibility.

I love when I meet with people; however, some people I meet with I know they have no revelation. I'm not mad at them, I'm not disappointed, I'm not putting them down. They just don't have any revelation. I can tell by how they talk to me. I can tell if they call me Pastor or not. I can tell a lot of things by how they open their mouth. I'm not mad at them, I love them, I'll still do anything for them, but I can tell where they are.

There are moments when I can meet with people where I can say just a little bit and they understand it. A sign of stupidity is when I have to explain it to you to the wall and back. The smarter you are, the faster you catch things. When you say someone is gifted (they don't use that word anymore), it used to mean that you had something above and beyond what everybody else has, you seem to get it faster than everybody else gets it. Do you realize that your measure of light is the same way?

When you're walking in low light, everybody has to sit down and tell you things you should already know. The more they have to explain for you to get it, the less light you're walking in. The more light a person has, when I recognize they have a lot of light, I'm concerned for them. When you have a lot of light, you're expected to walk in it. When you've only a little, it's easy. *If the one thing I have to worry about is this, I can do that. You tell me I have to love my neighbor? Okay, I'll do that. Then, I have to love God? I can do that. Now I have to love my enemy? You mean to tell me I have to love people who despitefully use me? Okay, I can love God, He loved me first. I'm good with that. I can love my neighbor; I like some of my neighbors, but you mean to tell me I have to love people who hate me? Then I have to forgive them seventy times seven?* Peter was like, "There has to be another way!"

The more light I have, now it's not just about loving God and loving my neighbors, now I have to love my enemies. I have to guard my mouth, behave appropriately. I can't live any old kind of way. Now I have light all over the place and I have to manage all of this light. That's why the apostle Paul said, "The things I do I don't want to do and the things I should do I don't do and the things I'm supposed to do I can't do" (Romans 7:19-20). He finished his course. You can't say that anybody walked in more light than this man did, and he wrote three quarters of the New Testament because he had so much light. Now you can understand when he said that.

Can you imagine having all of that light in which every decision in your life has to be measured against some portion of light? *"Can I just go do whatever I want to go do? Can I go sleep with whoever I want to sleep with? Can I be with whoever I want to be with? Can I go and act like I want to act? Can I go and hang out in the club? Can I go and hang out in the bars? Can I go and act like this on Facebook?"* All of these are areas of light in which God says, "This is how I want you to behave. This is how I want you to act because you are a light, not to be put under a basket but to be set on a hill so that the whole world can look at you and see the light in you."

APPLICATION OF LIGHT

Some of you, the reason why your friends walk in such darkness is because you're dark and you love talking about them. *"All of my friends, they're just in darkness."* That's because you're in darkness. If you were walking in light, you'd be a city on a hill, not under a bushel. Then when you pray and when you confess and when you decree, things start happening and people start paying attention. The church has been stripped of its power and the reason is because most of us don't want to do God.

A lot of pastors are afraid to teach messages like this because they're afraid you'll leave. I'm not. Here's the thing: If you leave, you've already heard it. You would have been better to have left before I even opened my mouth. Literally, it is what it is. You're putting the cart in front of the horse because it doesn't matter anymore. You have to know that the reason power is zapped out of a believer's life is because they do not walk in light. Any area in light you won't walk in, you will have no authority in. A tithe is ten percent and unless you made only $20, $2 is not a tithe. Ten percent—not nine, not eight, not eleven. Sometimes people think, *He's not going to tell me to give less.* Your tithe is ten percent; it's not eleven, fifteen, or twenty. Above and beyond that is your offering, not a tithe. You cannot give an offering until you've given a tithe.

If I understand that the Bible tells me that the Lord will open up a window of heaven and pour out a blessing that I will not have enough room to contain it (Malachi 3:10), He will protect my home, protect those things concerning me, and He will not let anything spoil before its time. If He's saying that based on your tithe, then if you're not a tither, don't come to me asking why you're struggling. What's the point? What do you want me to tell you? What answer would you like for me to give you? You want me to do some witchcraft. What do you want me to say? These are spiritual principles, walking in light. How can God move in an area in which you are disobedient? Some of you are waiting for the big time to come and the reason why the big time isn't coming is because you are not responsible with the little time. You're wondering why you get so close. Haggai says it's like you put money in a pocket that has holes in it (Haggai 1:6). If there's a hole in something, there's never enough. If your car is leaking oil, you have to keep putting oil in it because it's leaking out. Haggai is saying everything you have is falling out because you won't honor God. Then how do you expect Him to move in your finances?

If you're acting a fool in your relationships, why do you expect God to bring you a man or a woman? You don't even have respect. You're in the church looking at who you can sleep with and you wonder why your future husband or wife isn't showing up? You think God is stupid enough to damage them by giving them to you? This is what light is. When you walk in light, it opens you up to greater power of God and then you see greater manifestations of God. If I want to cripple the church, all I have to do is get you to not walk in light and let everything you do be with worldly principles, worldly love, worldly finances, worldly relationships.

The first thing I learned in ministry was to be careful of three things. They're called The Three G's: Gold, Girls, and Glory. Gold— money, be very careful about money. Don't let money run you, you run it. Money makes an excellent slave and a terrible master. Never be moved by the money. Girls—watch out for women. Women who are anointed, watch out for boys. Watch out for people because when you become anointed, when God's moving and you start walking in light, Satan will send people. They'll be just your type. They'll look just like you want them to look, but they're on assignment so you have to be careful of girls, and ladies be careful of boys. The last one is Glory—power. Be careful of glory because if you start to think it has something to do with you, you'll start believing your own press. As my mom would say, you'll start smelling yourself. You start thinking, "Hey, I'm anointed!" The moment you start taking your position for granted, Satan will tear you down. I've had people get very close to leadership and I've watched them go right back down again because it starts going to their head. They're not there anymore to make a difference in the organization; they're there because it's a position. *"I get to work with the pastor!"* Satan will literally tear them down because they missed it. I receive none of the accolades and I receive all of the correction. If there are accolades, it's Him. If I missed it, it was me.

When you understand that, then you will recognize the concept of light and how it applies in your life and how you have to walk. If we don't walk in light, if we don't allow light in our finances, money will rule us. We'll give when we have and only when we have. If we don't have light in areas of our relationships, we will be with everything that sparks our attention. If we have no light in the area of glory, we will seek after that which builds us up and not which builds God's kingdom. The higher you go, the more dangerous it becomes. If you watch every ministry that has failed, you will find that it failed because of one of those three things. Jimmy Bakker embezzled a large amount of money. They asked him how he did that and he said, "Because I was at the top and nobody was watching." Glory—thinking he didn't have to submit to anybody. He was the same person before; if you'll steal it at this level, then you'll steal it at this level. Why did he fall at this level and not at the other? If he was the type to just take money, you'd know that's who he was. Why would he do it? Your morals just don't change, but the higher you go, the greater the respect and responsibility you have to have for light. Because the same light that was there to help you, when it's misused, will be the same light that will trip you up.

WALKING IN LIGHT

"If we say that we have fellowship with him, and walk in darkness, we lie, and do not the truth."
—*1 John 1:6*

If you say that you have fellowship with God yet you do dark things, then He says you lie. In other words, you're not saying the truth because you do not the truth. You can say that we lie because we're saying not the truth. That would make more sense, but God says you're saying not the truth because you're not doing the truth. If I were to tell you right now that this portion of the ceiling is painted black, there are only two ways that I could be right. Either the color that I say the ceiling is has to be accurate, or I have to change the color of the ceiling to match what I said. A lot of times when you hear somebody say you're lying, what they are lying about is they're saying something that is false. They're not quoting the truth and you are usually able to say, "You're lying."

Notice here, it says that when you say what God says— light—you are saying the truth whether you do it or not. So what is required to change is not what you say. If the ceiling I say is red, in order for me to tell the truth, most of you would say, "You just need to say it's black." The problem with this scripture is it's not telling you that. It's telling you that if I say this thing is red, then I need to get up here and paint it red. In other words, what I do has to line up with what I'm saying. If I understand that the worlds were framed by the Word of God, whatever I say, if "I say unto this mountain, be thou removed, and be thou cast into the sea; and shall not doubt in [my] heart, then [it]...shall come to pass" (Mark 11:23), whatever I say, I shall then have. So if what I say is truly based on the light of God's Word, then it is not for me to back up or change what I say, it is not for me to do.

This is where people miss it. They are afraid to say. But how do we deal with scriptures that tell us God called those things that are not as though they were? The moment He said it, even if it wasn't, when it comes out of God's mouth, it now is. He cannot lie. What we do a lot of times is, we allow outward circumstances to cause us to back our mouth up. In other words, we just start backing up on what we're saying. This is the place where God says you lie. You're not lying when you call those things that which are not. Lying is when you call those things that are not, yet you won't do it. People think they just have to say what things are. No, you're lying when you're saying things that are not the light and the Word of God instantly. However, you are not lying when you call a situation different than what it is in light of the Word. I might struggle with some physical sickness in terms of my physical body, but you don't hear me saying that. If the Word calls me healed and whole, then I'm going to walk in the light of that Word. So if I walk in the light of that Word and you ask me how I feel, I feel great! If you ask me if I'm healed, I'm healed and whole. Venting is for people who have no prayer life.

This is the process people go through when they do not realize that you have to guard. If we're going to walk in light, then we walk in light. If you can get easily offended and it causes you not to walk in light, you are not in light, you're a liar. It isn't about what you say, it's about what you do. My ability to consistently walk in light means that I am able to regardless of the circumstances or the situation, I'm going to do the Word. As for me and my house, we are going to serve the Lord. When I understand that, I am obligated—despite my feelings, despite my emotions, despite what other people say—to walk this walk with God because it's a solo sport. When I stand before Him, He will not ask my friends about me. He will not ask my wife about me. When I stand before Him, He will ask me, "Why did you do these things when you knew better?" Because if you know better, you do better.

Sometimes Pastor Ricky will say this and sometimes when I travel with him I'll joke with him and say, "You need to stop calling my people stupid." He came here and he said something which was absolutely profound. He said, "If you don't know any better, you're ignorant, but if you know better and you won't do better, then you're stupid. Ignorant people we can help." You know how they say beauty is skin deep but stupid is to the bone. You have to recognize that ignorance is not so much the problem because when someone is ignorant, they don't know. This is why, for example, with denominations I don't have to be right. I can take all kinds of denominations and be all right with them because I can find a place to hook-up. If you teach denominationally the things of the full gospel, they'll hook up. They're not stupid, they just don't know. However, once you teach them, they will understand. There is nothing worse than full gospel believers who know but won't do. I'd rather go into a denomination church and turn that place out and watch the spirit of God fall.

Years ago, we were teaching at a Methodist church. The power of God was falling, people were getting healed, people falling out. Then we did a service and the pastor of the church was there. I'm like, "Lord, don't do nothing crazy please. They're going to throw us out of here." Next thing you know, people were falling out, getting healed, all kinds of stuff going off. The pastor came up to me and said, "That's one of the best services I've been in." I thought for sure they were going to shut it down. When the real true God shows up, it's not that they're stupid, they're ignorant. We have to be careful how we live our lives because you can either be stupid or ignorant.

God says if we say that we have fellowship with Him but walk in darkness, we lie and we do not the truth. Not that we don't *say* the truth, it's we *do* not the truth. However, "If we walk in the light, as he is in the light, we have fellowship one with another, and the blood of Jesus Christ, his Son, cleanseth us from all sin" (1 John 1:7). To walk in light, we understand that all light is not from God, but all God light is from God. Various people walk in different levels of light. Some of us might have a little nightlight and some of us might have one of them big old spot searchlights. Everybody walks in a different level of light. God doesn't tell you to covet somebody else's light. What He says is walk in the light you have and when you walk in the light that you have, you qualify for more light. Light is revelation, i.e., you get a revelation and you say, *"I understand now what tithing is about."* In Deuteronomy He tells us to tithe for one reason—to see if we'll put Him first. That's it. He wants to know if you will put Him first. Once you get a revelation of that, you can't back up.

There's this delicate balance and if any of you know me well enough, you'll know that when I see you walking in the light you have, that's when I start bringing more. Then you're like, *"Pastor, I just got this under control."* I know. The light shineth brighter and brighter unto a perfect (or mature) day (Proverbs 4:18). God desires us to mature, to continue to advance, and to continue to grow. Particularly, if you have a call of God on your life, you can't run from light as light will keep you when everyone else has forsaken you.

WALKING IN LIGHT

You have to recognize the value of walking in light. If you go to church just to soak stuff up, you want your ears to be tickled, you go because it's an obligation, you feel like it's the right thing to do and you're able to brag about the fact that you go to church, you've missed it. You are in boot camp.

I don't know what you're supposed to do. Sometimes I do, sometimes I don't. You might be explosive ordinances, you might be in a different branch, you might be in a different office. Here's what I do know, however: Everybody's being trained and developed. Once you have light on a subject, God expects you to walk in that light despite your feelings and emotions. When you have light, you also have truth. And when you have truth, you know what you should do. If you don't do it, James says that he who knows to do right but doesn't, to him that's sin (James 4:17). That implies that if he doesn't know, then it's not sin.

When you understand revelation, you don't need more money, you need more light. The faster you get the light you're walking in under control, then you actually qualify for more light. People don't understand that the reason they're not growing spiritually is because they're not walking in the light they have. I'll give you an example. Hypothetically, you have a boyfriend who's a nonbeliever and you want me to pray for you. Here's the problem: The Bible says to not be unequally yoked, adding, "What does light have with darkness?" (2 Corinthians 6:14). *"Well, you know, he comes to church and he's trying."* We don't try; we're not human *tryings*, we're human *beings*. We're either going to be it or we're not, but don't come ask me to pray when you have already violated the light you already have.

Some things are already written out, they're perfectly clear. I don't have to go to God to find out what He already told me under the pretenses that maybe by-and-by He will change His mind. *What I want to do* [which is outside of His will] *now I'm going to rope God into changing His mind to make what I refuse to correct.* Right? In other words, make my lie into truth. *What I'm trying to do* [because honestly, I don't walk in faith] *is not let go of one before I get another. I'm afraid that if I let go, I'll be alone.* Never forget this: God will always take you through a desert before He puts you into your promise. When He delivered the Children of Israel out of bondage in Egypt, He took them into a desert of solitude and a lack of supply before He took them into their promised land. Why? Because you can't act like an Egyptian in your promised land. You can't act like a fool. When you walk in the light that you have, when you realize, *"You know what? It might be difficult to separate from this unbeliever. It might even hurt my heartstrings, but if I do it and I walk in the light I have, then I have put God in the position to bring me the right person."*

One of my favorite old-time movies was "Trading Places." Eddie Murphy was a conman, a homeless street guy, and a couple brokers made a bet, based on an experiment to see what would happen. They said, "I bet you we can take him out of this environment, put him into a wealthy environment, and he'll completely change." So they took the guy who was wealthy, trained in the best schools, and broke him down until he was homeless. Then they took the homeless conman into a house and said, "This is your house now." He's like, "All of this is mine?" They said, "Yeah, this is yours." He said, "What about that over there?" As soon as they turned and looked, he grabbed something and put it in his pocket. He said, "How about that over there?" They looked that way and he grabbed something else.

Here's what they said, "You don't have to steal this stuff, it's yours." You can't take the hood into your promised land because you'll be in your promised land trying to steal, not realizing that it's already yours. So too in life. Every time God takes you to another place, He always takes you through a desert to strip you so that as you get stripped, you come out the other end ready.

Some of you, your attitude stinks and God's taking you through some things. Concerning your healing, some of you are wondering, *God, why won't you heal me?* You're already healed. You have to go into a desert place to be stripped of what your mama said, what your friends have told you, and what past denominations have told you. You are still trying to keep God in a box. If you don't get one thing but this, know that God does not fit in your box. God does not have a box; He's the Creator of all things great and small. It all belongs to Him. I hear many of you when you're in your wilderness experience gasping, *"It's dry here, Pastor. I've been here for so long."* It's because you won't wake up. The Bible says that the time it should have taken the Israelites to get from Egypt to their promised land should've been about 30 days. They spent years! Can you imagine what that must have been like—circling through the wilderness, passing the same rock five hundred times and seeing the same tree?

You know the saying, "You can take the brother out of the hood, but you can't take the hood out of the brother"? It took God that long to get Egypt out of them. How long is it going to take to get Egypt out of you? Life is the result of the conversations you have with yourself. If you don't find empowering meanings for things in your life, you will not value them. If you don't value light, then you'll sit through a message like this, think it's great, then get up and walk away.

The Bible says you'll behold yourself in the mirror, see yourself for a moment, then walk away and forget what manner of man you truly are (James 1:24). You'll go back to acting like the world, thinking like the world. Then you'll try to force your way into your promise, acting like an Egyptian. The truth of the matter is, the reason most people are not in their promise, why they're not seeing victory, is because they won't walk in light. They won't do what they know is right. Are they still saved? Sure. Will they still make it into heaven? Sure, but they'll live in hell all the days of their life.

Who wants to do that? Who wants to be stripped of our power? The Bible says all have sinned and fallen short of the glory of God (Romans 3:23). To fall short of something means that there was something higher and you missed the mark. It implies that God has a greater purpose for you. The glory of God is the power of God. It's not that you're not saved, it's that you won't see power. What's the point of jumping in a car that doesn't have any power? You might as well have a skateboard or a bicycle because you're the power of that. However, when you get into something and you expect there to be power, you expect there to be power. This is why Christians are living powerless lives because they think that they can mix sin with God.

When you start talking about these things, your hyper-grace people say, "You're making everybody sin conscious." I'm not making anybody anything. We are God-conscious, but we have to know that there is a formula to dealing successfully with God if you want to see the power. Now if you don't care about power and you want to live in hell all of your life, then help yourself. However, if you want to see the power of God, then you have to learn and obey the ways of God.

This is why the Bible says that the Children of Israel knew the *acts* of God, but Moses knew the *ways* of God (Psalm 103:7).

As a leader, when you're called to higher places, you can't just know what God can do—His *acts*—you have to know His *ways*. If you only know His act, then you are waiting, living miracle to miracle, waiting for Him. However, if you understand His ways, then you have the ability to flow in what He's already done. Now you're not waiting *on* Him, you are waiting *in* Him. There's a difference. This is where the struggle happens. *"God knows my heart."* That's why you should be nervous. What you say is not His issue. He didn't say, "You say not the truth because you said something wrong." He says, "You say not the truth because it's not what you do."

When Jesus is talking about the Pharisees in Matthew 23, He said, "Whatever the Pharisees tell you to do, do it, but don't do what they do." Isn't that something? If you noticed, Jesus had a hatred towards the Pharisees because they said one thing, but did something else. My concern is, how do we make it okay in our heads when we see Jesus hatred hypocrisy? He cursed the fig tree because it looked like it should have fruit but it didn't. He said, "No man shall ever eat from you again." That seems kind of extreme. How do we reconcile that he said, "You Pharisees are like white-washed sepulchers" (Matthew 23:27)? Let me put it into plain English. He said, "You Pharisees are like pretty coffins. You're shiny on the outside, but you're dead on the inside." He called them a "generation of vipers" (Matthew 23:33).

I can go on and on about the things Jesus said. So if God despises hypocrisy, how do we trick ourselves into thinking it's okay to do the opposite of what we say? How do we get there when He says, "I change not." Now, nobody's perfect so I'm not trying to put you in a position to be in guilt and shame. What I'm trying to do is bring you to a place of reflection to ask yourself if you're walking in light. Do you understand what it means to know what God wants, then to actually do it? The Word tells you to forsake not the assembling together of yourselves (Hebrews 10:25). What does that mean? Go to church. "Assembly"—that word is synagogue; the building. Not at your house; the building, the corporate worship where everybody comes together. Still, some people think it's okay not to.

How do we allow our emotions to wash light out of our lives? He said, "If , therefore, thine eye be single, thy whole body shall be filled of light" (Matthew 6:22). If your eye is not single, darkness will pervade the body. How great does darkness have to be to overcome light. How strong do your emotions have to be? How strong does your anger have to be, your lusts, your offense to get you to go against what you know God has said? Sin in its very nature is disobedience to God. What is in us that allows us to disobey what God has said and knowingly, willingly, do it anyway and still expect Him to love it? It's the sin nature. You haven't died. The Bible says, "I am crucified with Christ: nevertheless I live; yet not I but Christ liveth in me; and the life which I now live in the flesh I live by the faith of the Son of God, who loved me and gave himself for me....for if righteousness came by the law, then Christ is dead in vain" (Galatians 2:20-21).

You can frustrate the grace of God. All of these grace teachers get on TV and say, "You're okay, I'm okay, God's okay"— leading people straight to hell. How do we reconcile in our heads when we know that we can frustrate the grace of God? The apostle Paul said, "I dare not frustrate the grace of God, for if righteousness came by the law, then Christ was dead in vain" (Galatians 2:21). I can stop the grace from flowing in my life. If you're crucified with Christ, if you die, it's easy to walk in light. What causes you not to walk in light is that you will not die. The old man has to die. If the old man struggled with lusts, drugs, or alcohol, he has to die. This is the part of Christianity folks do not understand. They're trying to live with the old man and the new all at the same time. The Bible says put off the old man and put on the new, to get rid of the old and walk in the new (see Ephesians 4:22). When you walk in the new, all of a sudden the new man doesn't struggle the way the old man did. However, if you won't kill him, then he will keep coming back. People are walking around dead! If you won't kill him, he'll kill you.

When Jesus said the Pharisees were white-washed sepulchers, He basically was telling them, "You're just a shiny coffin. You're pretty on the outside, you're alabaster on the outside, but you're dead" (see Matthew 23:13). Now how do you walk in victory when you can't hear God? How do you walk in victory when you have light on the matter but your emotions convince you otherwise and cause you to respond contrary to the Word of God. The Bible tells you to love your neighbors (Mark 12:31). Love them. It also says that he who hateth his brother doesn't walk in light, he walks in darkness (see 1 John 2:9). How do we reconcile these thoughts? *"I don't like her. I just can't get along with her. I get along with other people better."* Okay. This is why you struggle; they're all unbelievers. If you were to be honest, if you get along with unbelievers better than you do your Christian family, then you should ask yourself if you are even a believer.

The Bible says what fellowship does light and darkness have? There are no secular people in my life that I have a greater relationship with than my church family. We don't even speak the same language. I've had people say things like this, "When your spiritual father comes in, do you pay him?" I said, "Handsomely, the best that we can and then some." They respond, "All that he's doing, he ought to just come do it for free." I wouldn't let him. Secular people don't understand that there's no way in the world

I'm going to let my spiritual father struggle. If he struggles and he's my supply... I'm not going to make anybody else walk in the light I walk in, but you're not going to change my light. I'm not stupid enough to back up. Whenever he comes here, we make sure that he leaves here blessed. Why? I want him to know that he's loved here.

Jesus said, "I know you honor your parents by your ability and willingness and execution of your support of them." The Pharisees said, "This is corban." In other words, they claimed they could not take care of their parents because all that they had was devoted to God. Jesus said, "You have rendered the Word of God of no effect by your traditions because you can't say all I have is God's and not take care of your parents." If all you have belongs to God, then the first thing God would do is take care of you, but they threw out corban because they were knowing that if they said that to Him, He would back off and let them have their money. Of course, they didn't realize they were dealing with Jesus. He said, "I know you honor your parents by how you handle things with them." I wouldn't let my father struggle. The oil was poured on the head of Aaron. The Bible says that the oil flowed from the top of his head, down to his beard, down to his tunic, and down to the ground (Psalm 133:2). The anointing starts at the top and it flows down.

I can say, "We're going to have a healing night." People I know that are sick won't show up. If I were sick and you told me you had a healing night, I would quit my job before I would not show up. I have flown across this country to be in a meeting that my spiritual father had because God told me to go. It cost me all kinds of money to get there, but I did it anyway. I'm not silly with my life. I understand that light is important. If I walk in the light that I have, if I'm going to be obedient to what God told me, then I act from a different perspective. People have asked, "You did all of that and you gave him all of that?" Yes, and that's why I walk in favor everywhere I go. You don't think that comes just because God thinks I'm cute. (He does, but that's not it.) Walking in light is the biggest problem that the Body of Christ suffers from. They know what to do; they just refuse to do it.

I was in a meeting one time with my spiritual father and he called out a word. I could tell he was struggling with it. He didn't want to say it; he even asked God a couple times, "Are You sure?" This is what he said: "There are some people in this room who know you're supposed to tithe and you won't do it. Because you won't do it, your children have acted up, your family has been under attack, you've been sick as a dog." The natural person would think, *"What does that have to do with anything?"* You can see why he struggled saying it. To say that would imply that everyone who is sick is not giving, which is not true. There are plenty of people who are not giving who are not sick, but in that particular meeting among that group of people, there were individuals, when he called them up, came because they knew it. God had already talked to them about it and told them, "Be not deceived, God is not mocked." We have to know that obedience in certain areas of our lives opens up blessings in other areas. How can it hurt to be obedient? How wrong can it be for us to obey God? What is it in us that thinks if we're disobedient, we can still move God?

If you're not eating the good of the land, if it always seems like there's just never enough, you have to check two things. Are you obedient? Do you do what you're supposed to do? Some of you might say, *"Pastor, I'm very obedient. I do all the stuff I'm supposed to do."* And second, are you willing? Most people forget all about the willing part. *"Well, I do what I have to do. If God tells me to do it, then I have to do it."* Willing means it's not what you *have* to do, it's what you *get* to do. Life is the result of conversations you have with yourself. I don't feel like I *must* come and preach, I feel as though I *get* to come and preach. I'm like a little kid, I just cannot believe that you would allow me to do it.

In my own mind, I'm an idiot. You might think I'm joking, but I'm serious. I've preached many times in front of crowds of several hundred and I've preached in crowds of ten. I'm always nervous. I can't believe that I get to! Sometimes I want to pinch myself. I'm like, "God, you really trust me?" This is a whole different world. I have butterflies in my stomach every time I'm on the platform. If you think it's the other way around, you've missed it. I don't go up there thinking I have it all together. I walk out there while praying, "Lord, don't leave me!"

When you deal with a healing anointing and you flow in a healing anointing, you come under greater attack than you do just preaching the Word. This is why it's fought so hard. If any of you believe you want to be used in a healing anointing, you had better be patient. You'll get out there in a place you should not be and Satan will eat your lunch. It's not easy. You have to know what it's like to have physical ailments in your own body, lay hands on other people, watch them get healed, and wonder why you are not. I've had those times. I've had those moments where I had to bring myself to a good place to minister to other people, and then go into my office and cry. You have to know the measure in which you're going to affect people's lives. If God has called you to a greater measure, you have to walk in greater light. What you won't do may not be what you can't do.

A friend of mine was looking for a place to stay and decided to move in with another brother from the church. They talked about the rules of the house and came to an agreement. This particular brother didn't have a TV in his house. God told him not to have a TV, saying, "The time you spend with the TV, I want to spend with you." So later on, my friend comes to me and says, "Man, I can't believe he ain't got no TV! Who has a house with no TV in it! This is ridiculous, I can't stand this!" I said, "Did you know he didn't have a TV before you moved in?" He said, "Yeah." I said, "Did you both talk about it?" He said, "Yup!" I said, "Then what's your problem? God told him something, it's not your place to judge, that's the light he's walking in. Your job is to see if you can walk in that light with him. If you can't, then you have to go." Of course he was done with me, so he went to vent to somebody else.

I can't be responsible for the light that you walk in, I'm responsible only for the light I walk in. The things God has told me to do I have to do. When I find myself in a place where I don't want to, then I remind myself that if I want to eat, then I put my flesh under and I make my want-to line up. I say, "Emotions, you will not run me. Feelings, you will not dictate this. We're going to do what we're supposed to do and I'm willing to do it. I don't *have* to do it, but I *get* to do it." So then I tell myself, *I cannot believe that God gave me the privilege to knock these edges off of him. I cannot believe He trusted me enough with his life.* Can you imagine the trust He must have? So now I'm willing and I'm obedient and I eat the good of the land. It's that simple.

Doing good is not doing God. I have watched so many people that should be in church walk away. They were attending, God healed them, they started walking in victory, and as soon as they left, things fell apart. Physical health, all kinds of things started to happen. That doesn't happen with all people. Some leave because they're supposed to leave. We're not a church for everyone, but we're a church for anyone. However, if you know where your supply is, you need to be where your supply is. That's where God moves.

Some of you have been in seasons where you felt like you've been on hold, then you go to church and everything speeds up. It's because earlier you were out of the will of God. Why all of a sudden would you speed up? You must be in His will. Why would you have greater resistance? You must be in His will. *"It was so much easier when I wasn't coming here."* I know, because you were no threat to Satan. None whatsoever.

There's a new term—"feel some type of way." Let's put our thinking caps on. Take it out of slang, out of what's common, and think about that statement. Good? Bad? Okay, well here's what I know. I don't allow myself to feel any type of way. I only allow myself to feel the type of way that is the God-type of way. So if my feelings don't line up, then I have to be willing before I'm obedient. If my feelings don't line up, I need more light on the subject. I will ask God what He wants me to do. If someone attacked me, they hate me, they talk bad about me, then they call me and need me, my response is "Hey! What can I do for you?" Why? The Bible tells us if we exchange good for evil, it's like heaping coals down the back of their neck (Romans 12:20). I've developed what I like to call "The Heaping Coals Ministry." That's where you can hate me all you want, but I'm going to love you and I'm going to pour out as much as I can. The more you hate me, the more I'm going to love you.

Love is infectious, powerful, real, and truthful. I can always overcome evil with love. Even when it doesn't look like I'm going to win, by staying and walking in love, I know that faith works by love. If I want my faith to work, then my love walk has to work. When my love walk works, then my faith works. If my faith works by love, then I can't afford to hate on you. I can't keep shelling out these ducats for the price to hate on you. I don't have the time nor the inclination. It is too expensive, so guess what I must do? I have to walk in the light I have. Why? I have too much to be responsible for to be able to say, "Uhh... well, thank you all for coming out here. Have a good night!" when I stand up to preach. I depend on God too much. When I have to walk in love, guess what? I have to walk in love. When I have to repent, I have to repent. When I have to change, I have to change. When I get correction, guess what I'm going to do? Correct. Why? There's too much riding on this. I need too much in my life to continue to do what God has called me to do.

Some of you have to be real with yourself and say, *"Look, I can't afford to hold on to the stubbornness, to keep shelling out this money for nonsense, to stay where I'm at right now, to hate my brothers and sisters. I can't afford the price of admission to walk in darkness. I have to walk in light because the light is free!"* In your light is your provision and you can't afford to let someone rob you of your anointing. You don't need more money, you need more anointing. You don't need more stuff, you need more power. You don't need more things, you need greater revelation; you need more light! If you have more light, you have more revelation, more understanding, more anointing, then you will walk in greater things and all those things you are going after will be added unto you. You don't have to chase after them, they're coming to you.

Jesus said, "Seek ye first the kingdom of God, and his righteousness, and all these things shall be added unto you" (Matthew 6:33). So many people are chasing after the blessing. Mine comes to me. He told me if I seek Him, all these things shall be added because my Father knows what I have need of. I just seek after Him. Some of you, when you're tired it's because you're chasing Him. The Bible says that out of the mouth of two or three witnesses is every word established (2 Corinthians 13:1). If I can prove to you in another place in scripture where the same thing occurs, then I have established what we would call Bible doctrine. The blessings of the Lord shall overtake you (see Deuteronomy 28:2).

This is why God told some of you to do certain things and you're trying to negotiate with Him. The problem is, He told you to go do it. Your provision is already there, but because you won't do it, you are waiting for it to come and it's already there. For example, let's say God said He wants you to start a business, but you say, "I don't have any money." He knows that. You have not told Him anything He did not know. He knew that before he said go start the business. He's just waiting for you to start. In the very nature of starting the business, He has already made provision. There's already somebody whose ear He's whispered into and said, *I know they don't qualify. It doesn't make any sense, but do it anyway.* When you step out in obedience, God is already there and He's already waiting. I'm talking about walking in real Christianity, the power of God, where He's before you in your life and all you have to do is walk in the light and do what He's asked you to do.

My prayer is always, "God, put me in the right place at the right time with the right people." You know how I know I'm with the wrong people? They act stupid. I know they're not godly. It's time to move on. Do I wish they would act right? Sure. You have to understand God is already there, He's just waiting for you to catch up. He's waiting for you to walk in more light. He's like a coach saying, "Come on, one more step! One more!" You're like, *"No! I ain't moving until Pastor smiles at me and so-and-so treats me right. I have every right to feel the way I feel!"* All because of your emotions and your feelers.

I was talking to my wife recently and said, "You know, one of the things I've got to learn and get better at is recognizing the presence of fear versus the absence of peace." We think, *I don't have peace about it,* but sometimes what we deem as an absence of peace is actually the presence of fear. This is where the inward leading of the Holy Ghost becomes imperative. I realized I hadn't asked God. The first thing I did that day was to repent and say, "Lord, what do You want me to do?" Then I went to sleep and in my dream He gave me the answer. I woke up at 5 a.m. and started working toward that answer. There was a moment where I was not walking in the light that I had. I had to bring myself to a place where I said to myself, "You know better. You're not attached to the outcome, you're attached to Him. So if He gives you the plan, that's the only plan that will work." I cannot take His plan, add my pieces to it, massage it and work it, and then walk out with my own plan and hope that He's going to bless it when He already gave me the plan.

LETTING YOUR LIGHT SHINE

We have to be greater containers of God's glory so that humanity may be helped. If you think it's someone else's job, you're sadly mistaken because it's your job. So many people sit back and talk about how they wish we had more ethical people and business leaders, and CEOs of companies. We place blame and responsibility upon established leadership. What I don't understand is why we don't recognize we have to build new leaders. Who's going to take these people's places? There's a system in this world called the Babylon system that's designed to be evil and foul. It's designed to hurt and cheat. We as Christians with our holier-than-thou thinking don't realize, "If it's meant to be, it's up to me." We have the responsibility not to criticize, but to change and grow and create the next wave of leaders so that this world can be affected. We can then truly be containers of His glory. If we get lost in the nonsense, the things that don't matter, our personalities, our own trivial issues, then we forget all about the fact that we are needed in the Body of Christ. The body is not just one person; it is made up of many members. It is a body that comes together and if you don't believe me, look at what twelve people who came together accomplished. They turned the entire world upside down. It doesn't take many, it takes unity.

The challenge for us as believers walking in light means that we need an understanding of what God says about us, what God expects from us, and then we have to walk in that. Some people are so emotional that their feelings dictate everything that goes on in their life. If they're having a good day, everybody's having a good day. You know how they say, "If Mama ain't happy, nobody's happy"? That's straight out of the pit of hell. Mama ought to be happy and Daddy ought to be happy. One person shouldn't upset the whole applecart. If our emotions are out of control and go unchecked, they can lead our lives into places that'll take us into darkness. Light tells us this is the way we're supposed to act, behave, and these are the things God expects from us. When we walk in darkness, we can say we're in light, but what we do is dark.

> *"And the city had no need of the sun, neither of the moon to shine in it, for the glory of God did lighten it, and the Lamb is the light of it. And the nations of them who are saved shall walk in the light of it, and the kings of the earth do bring their glory and honor into it."*
> *—Revelation 21:23*

John is saying in this verse that there's no moon or sun because the light comes from God and the Lamb. We understand Jesus is the Light. He says those who are saved won't need any light because they'll be walking in it. He says there will come that moment when the entire earth and all the kings will bring their glory and honor into God's light (see Revelation 21:23), and not the other way around because the highest level of truth is God's truth.

If you watch what is going on in society today, for some reason we are trying as the church to bring God's glory into man's glory. We are trying to fit God's light into man's light. We are trying to find ways to make it palatable by starting an underwater basket weaving ministry. We're trying to find ways to relate to people by the light of man and not the light of God. The challenge is that the church has no power because we have not truly stepped up and said we are not of the world, but are simply in the world. When I come to the world, I don't come to the world with the light that you have and try to explain to you my light. My light is brighter than your light. My truth is more truth than your truth. My reality is reality.

When you deal with people in the world, they think, *Oh, you're just in La-la Land. You're one of those Christians.* When you are burning in hell, you will come to the realization that there was a point in time when you should have heard what was being said. This is life and death. This is not a game, this is serious business. This is eternity we're talking about. I'm not going to argue with you over man and woman. I'm not going to shrink back and avoid talking about it. When's the last time you've seen a Christian pride parade? This is the challenge the church has because if we were to do that, then all of a sudden it's hate. What happens is, the world's light moves our light. In the real estate business years ago we used to say, "How did it go with that prospect?" If the person would say they didn't buy, we'd say, "They sold you, huh?" Somebody got sold and either you're selling them or they're selling you.

The light of the world is supposed to be brought into God's light, not the other way around. If I believe it's the other way around, when I approach darkness, I'm going to approach it with the conception that I have to bring in light that darkness has to accept. The only reason darkness can exist is because it's rejecting light, but God's light is still the truth. His light is still the right way. The Bible is the answer to all situations. My God is the real, true, one God, not Allah. We can't all just get together. If you fail to recognize Jesus Christ and Him crucified, we have nothing to talk about. *You know that's just closed-minded.* No, it's truth and I'm not going to try to bring my light and force it into the world so that the world can palette it. My light is the light from God and He is The

Supreme, The Grande Fromage, El Heffe Grande, The Chief, The Boss, The Beginning and The End. As far as I'm concerned, I don't have to bring my light into yours. You and the world are going to have to bring your light into His.

When you think about the times in which the book of Revelation was written, kings thought they were one step up as God. When you think about the glory of kings and why they would reference that to let you know that even if they believe they're God, they can redefine marriage and what we believe, there will come a moment when the light will be so bright, it will have to dwarf everything that stands in opposition to it.

We have light, but we're afraid. Think about the type of light it takes to be a martyr. In our current day, a martyr is not that common. You will not die or be murdered for what you believe, but when you look at the times of the apostle Paul, his job before he was converted was to kill and maim Christians. He was on a mission. When he went on the road of Damascus, he had just gotten papers that licensed him not only to clear Christians out of town, but to arrest and kill them. We don't have that today in America. We don't have to hide in caves or have Bible studies in tunnels like they do in some countries.

The problem is that the church has become soft. We've become fat and happy because all we want to do is sit in church and scream, "Come, Lord, come!" We've got all the rhetoric down, we've got all the posturing down, we've got all of the Christianese down. We've got all of the nuances down. We've got all of the things from the outside, but the truth of the matter is are we containers of light? Wherever we go, have we come out from the world and are we separate? Are we a light in dark places? When we show up, do people get nervous? When we walk into the room, does the devil say, *Wait a minute, who brought them? Who invited them?* When we show up at a family reunion, do some people walk the other way? The light in us should make people nervous. On the other hand, do people come to us and want to share their problems? We're thinking, *All I wanted was a soda and some French fries...* and all of a sudden they're revealing their intimate secrets. What we don't understand is there's light in us.

Some of you have been in darkness for so long, struggled for so long, have never seen the type of light that shines so bright that you don't need a moon or a sun, but you need the light of the One who shines in you. When you see that type of light, there's an attraction like a moth to a flame. There is something about you that has to be different. We want to play this pansy Christianity where we're "on the D.L." Someone once asked, "If being Christian was a crime, would there be enough evidence to convict you, or are you an undercover brother?" Nobody at work knows you're a Christian. People come in sick and struggling, but you don't say anything to them. *We're not allowed to talk about religion.* See, when you tell me what I'm allowed to talk about, you have forced your light over mine. The truth of the matter is, this little light of mine, I'm going to let it shine! I don't care if you like it or not, you'll just have to fire me. I dare you to do it. If you actually understood something, you would know that the fact I'm here is the only reason this company is still here. I'm not conceited, I'm convinced.

If the anointing is on your life—which I know it is—I know as a Christian what I'm telling you is a Christian is a little Christ. Christ doesn't mean "Jesus," Christ means "anointed." It means that the power of God is in your life. If you don't understand that you are anointed, appointed, and set aside for such a time as this, then you've let the world's light change your light. You'll walk in fear, you won't be able to step out with boldness and say, *"I don't care what you think about this. This is the truth and if you don't like it, then fire me and watch what happens."* When I set myself up to stand for God, He said if I won't deny Him, He'll never deny me. So I know that when I step forward with the boldness—I'm talking about boldness, not fear—*"Well, I don't know...we might not...."* Seriously? We have to know that we are coming into the end times.

I'm almost ashamed to admit some of the things we see nowadays. I have a reverential fear to even repeat some of the things that are happening. When have you ever seen such evil? Mothers burning and murdering their own babies! We are not surprised, but people are praying for world peace. Stop wasting your time because the Bible tells us that this is the time it's going to get darker and darker and darker. When will the church step up and stop worrying about vacations, going to the lake, about their possessions and junk? When will the church step up and say, "God, use me? Send me, I'll go! I'll say what you want me to say, I'll do what you want me to do. I'll live what you want me to live because I'm going to be a light for all that you are doing!"

What we need to do is start "mooning" people. The light of the moon is merely a reflection of the sun. When you see a full moon, the moon does not glow in and of itself; it merely reflects the sunlight. We need to learn how to reflect the Son Light so that when people see us, they see Christ in us, the hope of glory. When we show up, help shows up. When we walk in, things start changing. When we step into a house, every devil in hell starts running. All of a sudden when we show up, people feel refreshed. Some may feel angry at you; however, it's the same thing God told Samuel, "They're not rejecting you." If we're walking in our own reflection they're rejecting us, but when we walk in Son Light, they're not rejecting us, they're rejecting Him. When they're rejecting Him, it's a sad state of affairs because there will come that moment that His light will shine so bright, there will be no need for sun. There won't be need for a moon. It will be so bright that they cannot even hide from it. What about you?

Eschatology (a study of the end times) tells us in Thessalonians that until the Holy Ghost is removed, God is holding back Satan. When the church is raptured, then the Tribulation comes. When the Tribulation comes, the Bible says that as the church we have not been appointed unto wrath (1 Thessalonians 5:9). This means if you are a believer, you will not be here. When the Holy Ghost is pulled out, then Satan will be released. Even everything you go through now is being done from a distance. When the Holy Ghost is pulled out, Satan will be released. If the Holy Ghost is on the inside of you, then until you are raptured away the light on the inside of you holds Satan at bay. Your mere presence keeps him at a certain place and he will not have free rein until God comes and snatches you away. You need to let some people know that the reason Satan hasn't been released is the fact that you're here. Once you're gone, all of this stuff will go to hell. Here you're afraid to talk to them about Jesus, you're afraid to share the gospel with them; however, the fact that they enjoy what they enjoy is because you are here right now with them.

When you are gone, when you are taken out, that's when God will allow Satan free rein. That's why I don't have a problem with knowing who I am. The truth of the matter is I'm like, "You know what? I know you don't believe but you ought to thank me." Even if you aren't a believer, even if you worship rocks, whatever it is you do that's fine, but you ought to thank me as a Christian because the fact that the Holy Ghost dwells on the inside of me is the reason you haven't seen the fullness of what Satan can do.

All of the nations of them which are saved shall walk in the light of it and the kings of the earth do bring their glory and honor into it (see Malachi 3:12). They're bringing it into the glory and honor of God. Light always brings glory and honor to God. Palm readers, people with the crystal ball, say, "Your grandmama just came through and told me to tell you that she buried a ring in the north corner of the house and it's worth a whole gang of money." You run home, you dig up that corner, and lo and behold that ring is there. You're thinking, *Oh my God, Grandmama came and talked to me!* Grandma didn't talk to you, a familiar spirit spoke to you.

David said, "My enemies that observe me..." (Psalm 54:5 GW). Every family has spirits assigned to them that have been observing, watching, studying, and reporting what you do. This is why when people talk about things like generational curses, they think it's a generational curse, but a lot of it is the same harassment that came against your daddy. It's the same harassment that will come against you. It's the same spirits that have been there, so how do they know that Grandmama buried a ring? Grandmama didn't tell them that; a familiar spirit that watched Grandma do it told them. So when you deal with these mediums that read palms, crystal balls, and all this nonsense, it doesn't bring any glory or honor to God. That's how you know it's not God. Can they be accurate? Yes they can, but does it bring glory and honor to God or does it promote man?

All light that is true, God light, will always bring glory and honor to God. Are psychics real? Yes. Do they pick up things in the spirit? Yes. Are they of God? No. If you don't like it, so what. It's the truth. Whenever it brings glory to God, that's when you know God's in the middle of it. This is why light is so important to understand. He said their glory and honor are brought into His, not the other way around. God is not going to lower himself to fit in your box or to appeal to your mind. He's not going to lower himself to appease your emotions. God is God! His ways are higher than our ways. His thinking is higher than our thinking. His understanding is higher than ours. If you think you can force God to come down to your level, He is not going to do it. He is still God. Why? Because He made Himself God.

People have complexes. I don't care what you think, what does the Word say? The Word is the highest authority in our lives. If you say God told you something different, then you're a liar, because the Word and the spirit will always agree. God will not bend the rules for you. That's not God. God said, "I change not. I'm the same God yesterday, today, and forever." He does not change. Therefore, you have to understand our God is able. Sometimes we are very guilty of trying to take His light and force it into ours.

You don't know what I'm talking about until you have surrendered. Surrender is a whole different discussion. I can give up on life, I can just say, "I don't want to do this anymore, I'm tired, I give up." I can put a bullet through my head and be done. I can give up, but that's not surrender. Surrender is when I say to the Lord, "Okay, I give up. I can't do this no more. So here, I'm Yours." Surrender is not just giving up; it's to give up and to then turn over. When you understand biblical surrender, you say, "God, not my will but Your will. Not my way, but Your way. Not about me, but about You. I give it all up to You. I don't care what my life looks like anymore. I don't care what they call me. I don't care what they say about me. God, I'm Yours. All that I have is Yours. If You want it, You can have it all because You gave it all to me." That is surrender, when I die to myself and I say, "I don't care anymore; I don't care what people say anymore. I don't care if they like me or don't like me. I've been released. I've been delivered from people's opinions, their feelings. their fears and ideologies. I have been delivered!"

I'm not afraid to be bold. I'm not afraid to step up anymore. I don't belong to me anymore. When the apostle Paul stood before King Agrippa (Acts 26), he said, "Do you think it's an easy thing to convince me to be a Christian?" Paul said, "Everything about Christianity I would that you have except for these chains" (v. 29). When people leave your life, when those you love that are close to you are the ones who hurt you, when your friends turn their back on you because they think you're literally a nut, when you walk into a store, people don't like you but you haven't done anything to them, it's the God in you, the hope of glory that rubs them wrong. You're wondering, *What is the problem here? Why are simple things harder?* The world has set itself against you.

What happens when you say, *"I don't even care. I'm not attached to this stuff, you can have it. If you want it more than I do then you can have it."* I can tell you this much: My God is well able to do exceedingly, abundantly more than I can ask or think and I trust Him in that way. You want to know if you trust Him or not? Will you give Him what He asks you for? If He commands your life, will you give it to Him? Will you lay it down and say, "God, take it!", or are you just a quitter? Is it all about the job? Is it all about the stuff? *Pastor, you don't understand. I've got bills.* That's your problem, *you* have your bills.

I didn't call myself. If I'd have called myself, I'd have gave myself a different title. It'd have been Chief Grand Poobah of All Things Great and Small. You would have to roll my business card out like a scroll, but I didn't call myself. One thing I learned about surrender, when I surrender, now they have to feed me, house me, and take care of me. God doesn't run out on the bill. Some of you, the reason you don't see God moving is because you haven't completely surrendered. You gave up and committed spiritual suicide. There's a place of surrender where you realize that your life is not your own. What you want, think, and feel dies. You turn it over and ask, "God, what do You want?"

Here's the thing I want to help you understand. I had dreams, plans, things in my heart, an idea of where I would be by 30, 40, and 50 years old. I was moving up the corporate ladder and I was going to be a CEO. I was going to have things—houses, cars, boats, and planes. I had it all figured out. I was on the right track, I had gotten my assignment, and I said, "I'm going to go do it." I traveled all over this country. I had a plan and I was working that plan and making sacrifices for that plan. Then all of a sudden... *"God, You want me to do what? Yeah, I'm missing that. There's no way I'm hearing that right."* It required surrender.

Here I was in church (which probably didn't have more than 20 people in it at any moment in time) and I had invited a friend to come. He had no church experience to speak of, it was more Catholicism (I'll specify why that's important in a minute). It was a Sunday night, my pastor had an altar call, and he went forward. I was the head usher. I'm standing off to the side, waiting to see what happens. My pastor lays hands on him, he falls out, and my ushers are going in to do the catch. Now, he has no frame of reference for that. I understand that, but coming from a Catholic perspective, when is the last time you've ever seen that? He was so scared that as he hit the floor, he tried to jump back up as if somebody punched him. I could tell that he was shocked and that he had a moment with God.

I'm working in the corporate world traveling all over the country, making boatloads of money, money longer than train smoke, and God said to me, "That's what I want you to do." I said, "Yeah, okay, let me tell You something. I've been around my pastor a long time. People treat him wrong; they say they love him and they'll leave in a heartbeat. They treat him with absolute disrespect. As long as they're happy with him, they love him. When they don't love him anymore, they're done with him. Your people are mean, they're like herding cats. I'll go into the secular world, I'll make a boatload of money, and I'll funnel it into the kingdom. That'll be my contribution. Dealing with Your people, I ain't going to do that." I started crying, sobbing uncontrollably.

Here I am, everybody sees me as a leader, I'm a professional, I have it all together, and I was bawling. I don't mean tears, I mean that nasty, snotty bawling. So I thought, *Okay, let me get out of here because I've got a reputation.* I walked a few buildings down away from the church and stood in front of one of them. My pastor came out, I could see him off in the distance looking around and he saw me. He walked up to me and said, "Until you say yes, that will never stop," Then he walked away. Now I was thinking, *How does he know what was said to me in the first place? Second of all, who's running service?* I was the head usher, I was mission-minded. Even in my own dysfunction I was concerned about what was going on. So finally, standing on the corner of 32nd Street and Thunderbird, I said, "Okay, I'll do it."

For the first three years of pastoring my church I was paid nothing. I had to close my companies so I didn't have anything else. For three years God sustained me, He sent the ravens to feed me. In the natural, it would have been easy to say, "I'm not doing this. If You show me how I can do it, if You give me a job that lets me be flexible...if You set it up so I can...if You would just show me how, if You would just let me in..." There is a point when you surrender, you don't know what you're surrendering to. What you do know is whatever you have surrendered to is better than where you came from. You realize that you had it all figured out, but it didn't matter because what you wanted was not what God wanted. When He takes over, He gives you provision for the vision. There is a future, a hope, an expectancy, a love that comes and a peace that surpasses all understanding. Today, I have more peace than I have ever had in my entire life. It all came from saying yes.

I didn't know where provision was coming from but I said yes. I didn't have all the answers, didn't know if I was going to make it, but I said yes. I came to the realization that God is trying to get a hold of some people and He will not take no for an answer. You don't have a choice but to serve Him and follow Him. There is something deep on the inside of you that is shut up in your bones. I'm not talking about pansy Christianity. I'm trying to be a general in the army. I want all guns pointed at me. When I show up on the battlefield, I want the enemy to go, "That's him right there. We take him out, we take out a whole bunch."

We get the Christian rhetoric down, but Christians are getting their butt whooped. I know that when I stand with my shoulders squared off, I know it's not me, it's He that is in me. When I say "Greater is He that is in me," I mean greater! What about disease, poverty, lack, or poor relationships? Greater! Whatever it is, the God that's in me is greater than he that is in the world. The light that is in me is greater than the light that is in the world. When I show up, He just showed up. He said, "Wherever you put your foot I have given you that the kingdom of God is on the inside of you wherever you go" (Joshua 1:3). When you show up, the kingdom has just showed up with you. Wherever you go, the glory has just showed up with you. I don't care where it is, you should be able to go into the strip club and shut it down just with your presence! You should be able to just drive by a bar and say, "Close in the name of Jesus" and shut it down.

When we were talking to the people at our last building, I told them, "If you put us in here, you will find that this place will start to fill up." It did. Then they started to deal with us in a pretty poor manner and it went back down. When we first moved in there and they were doing right by us, people were moving in and taking up space. They were prospering because they took care of us. We negotiated for a year for our new building, and I told the guy, "You will never lease this until you talk to us." He said they had others who were interested, they were going to pay a year in advance and had hundreds of people. I said, "Okay."

There are two ways to see what a T-bone steak looks like. One, you can ask the butcher and he'll tell you. The other, you can stick your head up a cow's behind. I don't recommend the latter, but I do recommend the former, it's much easier. Some people just have to figure it out the hard way. When I said "Okay," I'm sure he hung up the phone and said, "Who does he think he is?" He missed it. He had the right question, but he had the wrong subject. It wasn't, "Who does he think he is?" It was, "Who does He think He is?"

I have learned that when you stand for God, He will stand for you. Think about Stephen when he was being stoned. At the time, Saul (later the apostle Paul) was murdering Christians and he's was enjoying it. Now he's watching Stephen being stoned. The Bible says that as he was being stoned, he looked up and saw Jesus standing. Whenever you see a historical account of a king, he will always be seated on his throne. When someone approaches, the king will raise his scepter to say, "Come." That gives them permission to approach. A king will only stand to greet someone when he deems them as equal.

This is the only account you will read that Jesus is standing, almost to say that as you are being stoned for Him—because of the persecution you are going through—it now puts you and Him equal. There are plenty of people who died who were believers and Jesus said, "Come on in." However, when He sees someone who had to put up with some junk, get attacked, take some stones, give up their life, and die for the call, He had to come up out of His chair. He sees something that He doesn't see in everybody else. He sees you are different and you are truly reflecting Him.

Will you die for the call, or is it a party? Is it just something you do? I want Him to stand when I show up. Call me crazy, call me selfish, but if He did it for Stephen, if He was that proud of him, I want Him to be that proud of me. Was Stephen perfect? No, but he gave his life for the call. Was he the best guy that ever walked the planet? No. How many books of the Bible did he write? None, but it said that as he was yielding up the ghost, he saw Jesus standing, waiting to receive him.

What about the world you're coming out of and the world you're about to go into? What about the place where you long to be versus the place you're supposed to be— the place where you now are looking at your desire versus your destiny. You're looking at what is behind versus what lays ahead. You want to be back there because that's what feels good, but if you stay there, you'll get stoned, and it hurts. Now you're in that place of transition. You're trying to figure out how to truly surrender.

Jesus is standing, saying, "Come on. Well done, thou good and faithful servant." That means when my family, friends and church members talk about me, I don't care. You want to know why? I play to an audience of One. I'm not here to please you, I'm here to offend your mind and reveal your heart. I'm not here to be your pal or your buddy. I'm here to pastor, to point towards Him and say "That's the way." Will I make mistakes? Of course, but guess what? A righteous man falls seven times but he gets back up. We're going to make mistakes, stumble and falter, but we're going to get back up and we're going to keep chasing Jesus. That's why Paul said, "Follow me as I follow Christ. The only way you're following me is if you're following him" (see 1 Corinthians 11:1).

Most people use softeners; they find different ways to say things to make themselves feel better. *I ain't fat, I'm big-boned. I don't drink that much, I'm a social drinker.* We license ourselves by our own thinking because it sounds better. *Well, God's working on me.* Are you sure? If He was working on you, it should be shut up in your bones, you can't stand to miss the mark. There should be something in you that just cannot fathom the idea of disappointing Him. If God's working on you, then nothing takes precedence over Him. Not a husband, a wife, mother, father, child; not a job, school, money, things—nothing.

Nobody talks about these things anymore. Again, we try to put world into the church. We try to change God to fit the world. People say things like, *"Well, if God was around today He'd have written the Bible differently."* I'd rather hear a mule braying in a tin barn than to listen to such stupidity. I don't know what God you know, but my God is the God of Abraham, Isaac, and Jacob. My God is the one who split the Red Sea, who makes a way when there is no way, who has all the answers. He is Jehovah Jireh, El Shaddai. He's my peace, He's my joy, He's my victory, He's my banner, He's my health, He is Alpha and Omega. He is the First and the Last, the Bright and Morning Star. He is the Rose of

Sharon. I don't know who you're talking about, but I don't have a God that was; I have a God who was, who is, and will forever be. I don't know who you're talking about, but the One that I know said, "I change not." It worked then, it worked now, and it'll work in the future because God is real. His Word is pointed and sharp! You better get out of the way before I cut you.

It is what it is, and many a person has tried to change it. I remember years ago, it was easy to convert a Jehovah's Witness because they used our Bible containing things that contradicted their doctrine. If you knew these things, when they came knocking on your door, they messed up. But in the late 80s, they rewrote the Bible to exclude those parts. Why? Because they wanted to bring their light to overshadow *the* Light. If you notice, there are a lot of African Americans and Asians involved in the Seventh-Day Adventist Church, founded by Ellen G. White, a racist. When you read about her, what they will say about her is that she was the lesser light pointing to the greater light. They built an entire denomination built on lesser light. If you don't believe me, go look it up for yourself. I am not the lesser light pointing to the greater light; I am reflecting *the* Light. I am nothing but a mere piece of glass. If you trollop me underfoot I become sand; nothing. However, when I reflect His light, and all that He is, I am not lesser anymore.

You hear people say, "I'm just a sinner saved by grace." Maybe you are, but I *was* a sinner. My righteousness is filthy rags; I was absolutely the scum of the earth. The moment I accepted Jesus as my Lord and Savior, the Bible says that substitution occurred. Now my righteousness is of Him and I'm made right-standing because of my faith in Him. If I thought I was lesser light, then I would try to earn to become greater. I cannot become greater. All I can do is reflect greater degrees of His light. I'm not building a denomination around what I believe and think. I don't know anything, period. I'm as dumb as a box of rocks, but when it comes to God, I know Him and I endeavor to walk in greater light. As I walk in the light I have, I qualify for more, and I get to step up to greater light.

What do I long for? I long for that day in Revelation where John says there will never need to be a sun, there will never need to be a moon because all the nations of them which are saved shall walk in that light. Can you imagine the day when you have all of the answers, where you are walking in such light that you don't need a sun or a moon and God reveals it all? Now you can bask in the light and feel the warmth on your face, be in His presence where you're actually at the feet of Jesus and you can feel it.

You know why people act crazy when there's a full moon? It's the same reason the ocean tide comes in and out. The body is made up of 90 percent water. There's something about the moving of the moon that moves the water. It disturbs people who are flesh-driven. If you're spirit-driven, that doesn't matter. Can you imagine what happens when all of your fabric and being is in the light of God and you're in your glorified body? The same way the moon moves, can you imagine what that's going to do, not to your flesh because you won't have any, but to your spirit? I'm trying to get you to see something that you can strive towards and realize that it's greater than this. It's greater than opinions, laws, and presidents.

I've never seen a president more disrespected in all of my life than the one in office now. I don't know if it's because of his race because I think this is where the world is going. It might have something to do with it, but I don't know that's all of it. The world is getting more disrespectful; honor is a lost thing. If you can't see the times we're in, you are blind. The problem is when you see the times we're in, you have to know what that's telling you. It's telling you business as usual is not going to work any longer. God is saying, "I need some of you to stand up and be accounted for, to let your allegiances be seen." I am on God's side, not the world's side. I'm not going to sit in the middle, I'm going to make my position known with boldness. I don't care what happens to me, I don't care what they do to me, I don't care what they say about me.

If you're moved by what people say, you have some growing to do. The truth of the matter is, if people are not talking bad about you, you are not doing anything. We have a mission and a purpose. Who's ready to say, "Send me, Lord." Don't say that if you aren't serious, don't even let that come out of your mouth if you're not serious. Are you ready to say, "Send me, Lord, I'll do it. I'll say it, I'll be Your mouthpiece." If you think He's going to tell you just to say nice things, you've missed it. Sometimes you have to say the tough things, but if you're ready, genuinely ready, then I want you to say this: "I'll go, I'll do it, I'll submit. My life is Yours, I surrender. I give up, I'm waving the white flag. I've tried it my way, and it didn't work. Your way, Your will only. I'll do it. In Jesus' name, amen."

COMING UP TO LIGHT

Dad Hagin used to say that it's dangerous to come up to light and then walk away. Once you have light on a particular area or matter, God expects you to walk in it. We have entered into a dispensation of time, in my opinion, where people have become extremely lax about the things of God. We have this kind of hyper-grace stuff being propagated that gives the impression God is okay with disobedience and He doesn't expect you to do anything He's asked you to do. Of course it's unpopular to teach and talk about God having expectations upon your life. A lot of pastors steer clear of it because they're afraid you'll leave. The truth of the matter is, the only one I'm afraid will leave is God. I want Him to stay. If He stays and you go, then as the old saying is, "Then those are the breaks." The reality is you should stay and He should be able to stay. We should be able to grow together and walk in light.

We understand that light is revelation, illumination, clarity, and understanding concerning the purposes and will of God. When God's will becomes clear in your life, He expects you to walk that out. So many people have compartmentalized God into a box and say, *"Well, that's just my church life."* Their church life does not reflect their work life, and their work life does not reflect what they've learned in church. We don't even want to get into social life because now the social life doesn't reflect what was learned in church either. We think that they are very distinct things and then we wonder why people have problems with the church. They say things like, "The church is hypocritical"—which it is. People are frauds and they're faking. When people say things like that, what they're saying is what they see in church is not what they see in your personal life. Therefore, they call that hypocritical.

If you know anything about Jesus, one of the things He talked about on a regular basis is hypocrisy. Jesus hated that. Either you're in or you're out. Listeners said, "We're going to bury him, then we'll come follow you." He said, "Let the dead bury the dead." Who says things like that? I think we miss it because we want to make ourselves feel better about things. However, when you hear something like "Let the dead bury the dead. If you're going to follow me then follow me" (Matthew 8:22), how do you get there? When you hear Him say things like, "I didn't come to bring peace, I came to set mother against daughter, father against son, husbands against wives" (see Matthew 10:35) what do you do with that? Where do you file that piece of information when he said, "I didn't come to bring peace." He said, "I didn't come to make people get along, I came that when people follow Me, other people are going to get mad. I came to destroy and tear apart what isn't of Me. So if husband and wife can't follow me, I'll tear that apart." What do you do with that?

We have this candy land, ooey-gooey Christianity that says everything is okay and God's all right with us not being all about Him. We can live our lives in separate compartments; we can have our church lives, then be in here putting on the front. We've got all the Christian rhetoric down and all the different worship poses. When we've been in church long enough, we've seen them all. I think we've learned how to practice Christianity but I don't believe we've learned how to function as Christians. When you practice Christianity, it doesn't matter whether you go to church, make it to service, fellowship with your Christian brothers and sisters, or if you love one another. You can just be as hateful as you want to be, as disrespectful as you want to be, and think it's okay because they have to forgive you. Yeah, you're right, but that doesn't mean they have to tolerate you.

It's so bizarre to watch how people see and view Christianity. They almost see it like it's a hobby. However, if it were a football game, they would be painting half their face one color, screaming to the point where they lost their voice and show up at work on Monday where they can't talk. Then they get into church, praise and worship is going on and you can literally hang your jacket on them. If God is all for you, if you don't know that it takes all that, then you don't know God and you haven't met Him yet. When you meet Him in a place where there was no choice, when you have nowhere to go and have nothing, all of a sudden you get a grand appreciation for the God which we serve. When He becomes real in your life, when you actually understand that He truly is the author and finisher of your faith, that He truly is the beginning and the end, when it becomes all about Him, strap in.

I've heard people say it's easy to be a Christian. It's not easy being a Christian; it's easy to be in the world and go to the bar. It's easy to party like a rock star. I never had such resistance in all my life as I did when I decided to serve God. There was no resistance going to the club. Nobody had a problem with that; everybody wanted to go. Nobody ever said to me, "Hey, you know, you go to the club too much. You might not want to drink every time you go out. You mean to tell me you're going to go to that bar and give that man your money?" They never made these statements. Then I started going to church. "You're always in church!" I could think of worse places to be. "I can't believe you're going to go in there and give that man your money." You are not giving this man anything. What are we going to do—buy a Bentley with that $2 you gave? Quit it, it doesn't even make any sense.

The reality is, it's such a struggle when you move to a place of saying, "I'm going to follow God and serve God. It's going to be all about Him." When I say *all* about Him, I mean ALL about Him. I've never seen more flakiness than I have in the Body of Christ. Secular people can stay on track. When's the last time you've seen Christian Anonymous? We don't need 12 steps to get out of church, we need one. I don't know anybody who has to go on any type of medication to bring you down off of church. When you think about it in some of these contexts, you think, *Really? Why am I fought so hard?* Satan does not want for you to come up to light. Once you come up to light, you come to a place of understanding that now you get a reality and clarity of what God wants to do in you and through you.

There are different types of people. There are people who are called (that's you), and people who know they are called (which might not be you). All of you are called. The question becomes, do you know it? Then the people who know it are broken down into two categories—the people who will and the people who won't. Here's the beautiful part about it: You're going to get attacked either way. The one who won't is going to walk in the same, if not greater, attack because of their disobedience than the one who will. The misconception is that the one who will say *"Well, I just serve God"* will never be attacked. The devil is a liar! This creates a problem. *Now what do I do? If I do, I get attacked. If I don't, I'm attacked.*

"Pastor, you're not building a very good case." I am, just hang on. The difference between the ones who will and the ones who won't is that the ones who will have answers and the ones who won't, don't. They're still trying to figure it out.

I learned something a long time ago about taking a test. If I know the answers to the questions, I pass. My tests are what lead to my advancement into the next level of my life. I've seen so many people who feel stuck, but they're stuck because they have not passed the test. I remember when I was in high school, some of the football/basketball players, high-profile kids, passed whether they were smart or not. You watched them advance from grade to grade dumber than a box of rocks. They were passed because they had something to contribute other than their intellect. When administrators needed their skills to advance the school program, then they bent rules in order for them to pass. The problem is God doesn't need anything from you, so He'll leave you in first grade and you'll keep failing the same test. I've watched people get into a relationship, it goes south, and they come out of the relationship. Then they choose a guy or girl just like the other one. I made a list and I said this is what I can't stand. I can't tolerate this, I'm not willing to tolerate that anymore. This is what I don't want and what I do want. My God is faithful because He gave me everything on my list.

I don't have a problem making the same mistakes. If I bang my head against the wall, I don't want to stay in the same spot, I need to move over. I don't care if I have holes all the way down the wall. What I have a problem with are folks who keep banging their head against the same issue, the same wall, the same problem, the same challenge. *I feel like I'm stuck.* You are, you're stuck doing the same thing last year and the year before. *I just don't know how to pull myself out.* Well, here's the thing. If you're 30 years old and you're still in first grade, you're the only kid in the class that shaves. The premise of insanity is that everyone else is wrong.

I read something on Facebook that was pretty funny. A pastor friend of mine in another state said, "A pastor comes to you and tells you what you should do with your life. You tell him to mind his business, but you'll go spend money and hire a life coach, can't wait to give them your money and are super-excited about everything they tell you to do." Isn't that bizarre? This is the mindset of people. The challenge we have is how do we walk the way God wants us to walk? The only victory we'll ever experience is when we do this God's way. The only real truth is God's truth.

We have learned over the years to accept whatever has been given to us. It comes by media—print, television, music, and internet. All of these devices and mediums of expression have found their way into our lives in order to redefine what we believe to be truth. Studies have been done with the younger generation being brought up today where they say they don't even believe in marriage anymore. There was a time when a young man getting into his upper teens and early twenties was looking to find a wife. A young woman had dreams of being a wife, and it was about finding each other. Nowadays, it's all about how do we sleep with each other? Then, we'll come to church to do it. You know you have to be a special kind of brazen.

How do we bring ourselves to a place of recognizing that worldly things and godly things are very different? I have Pandora on my phone. One day in the car I was trying to find a Christian music station. It's hard because it either goes from one extreme where everybody's dying and saying "Jesus, save me" (which is just depressing), or it's the other extreme. I created a Mary Mary channel and they had a song by R. Kelly called "Prayer Changes Things," or something like that. I hit the button—next! How do we get that onto a Christian channel? I don't know if you see it sometimes the way I see it, but I see it as an overt attempt to derail us. This is where the world is right now. God is looking for some people who are going to step away from the world and say they're going to live for Him. I don't care how you slice it. If you play in the world and you're playing with God, He calls that being a whore. I have a problem with thinking of myself in that way, especially if I'm not getting paid.

> *"But God has revealed them unto us by his Spirit; for the Spirit searches all things, yea, the deep things of God. For what man knoweth the things of a man except the spirit of man which is in him? Even so the things of God knoweth no man, but the Spirit of God. Now we have received, not the spirit of the world, but the Spirit who is of God; that we might know the things that are freely given to us of God. These things also we speak, not in the words which man's wisdom teacheth but which the Holy Spirit teacheth, comparing spiritual things with spiritual. But the natural man receiveth not the things of the Spirit of God; for they are foolishness unto him, neither can he know them, because they are spiritually discerned."*
> —*1 Corinthians 2:10-14*

On the inside of you, you have your human spirit. For the sake of this discussion, we'll say it's your conscience. The voice of your conscience is the Holy Spirit. Every one of you who has been born again, your spirit has been reborn on the inside of you. When your spirit is reborn on the inside of you, God put His Spirit on the inside of you with your spirit. So now what knows the man better than your spirit? Your spirit is you.

Not to be morbid, but if there were a casket with a body in it, if you pinched it, kicked it, dropped it or whatever, it wouldn't respond because there's nobody home. The spirit has left that body. What makes you alive is the spirit on the inside of you. So you are a spirit, you live in a body and you possess a soul—your mind, will, and emotions.

First Corinthians 2:9 says, "Eye hath not seen, nor ear heard… the things which God hath prepared for them that love him." How do you not know by your eyes or your ears? Your natural senses cannot discern all the things God wants to do. You can't even know the full plan of God for your life without having the inward witness of the Holy Ghost, not the outward witness of your eyes. Not the inward witness of yourself because you want it so bad. I'm talking about the inward witness of the Holy Ghost, God, on the inside of you that speaks to your spirit. Not in a natural way. *But I'm lonely.* Get a dog. They're cheaper, trust me. They don't talk back and five minutes later they've forgotten everything you said.

Paul is telling us we compare spiritual things with spiritual things. If you don't have the understanding of God leading you, then you'll compare fleshly things with spiritual things. You'll run around looking for a sign. You'll ask God to make a red bird fly across the sky. Here's the challenge: Satan can make that red bird fly across the sky, hoping that you are so in tune with your flesh that he will use fleshly things to get you to move. Fleshly things will speak volumes to you, as opposed to the Spirit of God which is that still, small voice that says, "Don't do that; leave her alone; don't mess with him; don't take that job; I wouldn't do that." Satan presses people's buttons so next time you're around them they do the exact same thing again. Now you've gone from 0 to 60. You're comparing spiritual things with natural things.

If I had to compare spiritual things with natural things, I would have shut this ministry down a long time ago. I was not paid for years on end, not knowing where my next meal was coming from. I had to have a yard sale to put food on my table. I sold things I worked hard to own. People don't understand what many pastors actually have to go through. If I had watched the natural things I'd have said, "You know what? I'm going to do something else. I've got plenty of talent, skills, ability, and I'm smart enough and, gosh darn it, people like me." So why in the world would I stay doing something that has no value to me unless there's a still small voice inside to say, "Keep going, son. You're going to be all right."

Even now I'm concerned how people see it when I have nice things. I ask myself, "Do I deserve that?" Then I think, *Yeah, you know the three years I didn't get paid? I deserve it. When I stuck with this when people left, I deserve it.* There were people who were happy to see my ex-wife go because they thought it was their opportunity to step into my life. When they found out it wasn't them, they left. "Glad to see you go!" If you're going to serve God, you can't compare natural things with spiritual things. What God is doing in the spirit realm doesn't always line up with what you see in the natural. However, what do you do when you have to give up your 4,000-square-foot home that you bought because you loved it? Now you have to give it up and still serve God. Now you have to depend on the kindness of strangers and still serve God. Now you have to have a yard sale and then you have to tithe off a yard sale. You have no idea the stress that is induced in your life when you have to figure out where your next meal is coming from.

Some of you have been in that place, but it's amplified as a man. You question your ability to be a man. You wonder if this a problem to solve or a tension to manage. You have no idea what that's like to not even know. That's why when you hear people say things now, "Pastor, you sure have some nice clothes. You sure drive a nice car. You sure got nice stuff." I'm like, "Seriously? Let me take you for a walk with me." When everybody would have given up and I didn't, when everybody would have thrown in the towel and I didn't, when I'm getting rid of all of mine so I can make sure all of the church has a place to come and worship. This isn't for me; I'm not the one being taught. I know what I know.

The whole reason I'm telling you this is because there are some of you going through situations right now, and you don't understand that it's because you've made a decision to serve and to follow God. When you compare natural things to spiritual things, that's when you get into comparison with the Joneses and you start thinking, *How come they don't do nothing for God but yet they still have?* I don't care what they have. What you have to go through is that testing period, that breaking period. God wants to know, do you love Him when you're single? Do you love Him when you're married? Will you love Him when you're broke or when you have money? It doesn't matter about the stuff. What matters is your heart and He wants to know, will you stick with it? Will you ride it out or will you run?

Who knows the man like the spirit of man, and who knows God like the Spirit of God? He said only the Spirit can search the deep things of God. Only the Spirit can give you the answers you're looking for and bring resolutions to problems. God can give you an idea that will solve the whole situation and take the company to new levels. God can give you one idea, but it's only the Spirit of God who searches the deep things of God. When you are up against the wall, you'd better be able to hear that Spirit saying "Keep going."

God moved me into a position where for four years I lived in a house rent-free. You want to be up, but you don't want to climb. Everybody wants to go to heaven, but nobody wants to die. There's a price to pay and God wants to know if you are moved by the stuff. Are you comparing natural things with spiritual things? Comparing doesn't mean you evaluate, because you should evaluate natural and spiritual things, but woe be unto the person who compares the two. When you start comparing, that's when you start looking at paychecks and thinking, *"I know I want to serve God and the church needs help but I've got to have a paycheck."* What you've said, in a nutshell, is that *"God can't prosper me in any other way that I can't do."*

Coming up to light is deeper than just having understanding. In all our getting we get understanding. Do you not think there were nights where I laid in my bed saying, "I'm not sure this is going to work. God, I know what You called me to do but You've made a mistake." You don't think there were nights where I've said, "God, you're a liar. You told me You'd take care of me, You told me You'd meet every need. Here I am preaching and telling everybody You're a good God and You're not helping me. I'm fighting every angle of my life." When I reached that place, you know what I was doing? Comparing natural with spiritual things.

> *"Now we have received not the spirit of the world but the Spirit which is God that we might know the things that are freely given to us of God. Which things also we speak not in the words which man's wisdom teacheth, but which the Holy Ghost teaches comparing spiritual things with spiritual."*
> —*1 Corinthians 2:12-13*

There are flows to God. Let's say we're in a church service together, and my spiritual father is in this room. Someone begins speaking in tongues. I would stop and refer to him first to see if he had the interpretation. Why would I do that? He's the highest flow in the house. If you notice when the Bible talks about an interpretation of tongues, it doesn't say "*the* interpretation" it says "*an* interpretation." (1 Corinthians 14:26). That means there could be multiple interpretations. Let's say he doesn't have it. The second highest flow in the room would be myself. Let's just say for the sake of this discussion that someone else jumped up and said, "I got it!" I know I have it, so I'm going to tell that person to sit down. Their interpretation isn't wrong, but it's not the highest flow. What they wanted to say would edify the body and it would be on point, but it would not be the highest flow.

Why do we do praise and worship? Why do we have corporate worship? Corporate worship is to take the Body of Christ in. Say I can only take an individual to a certain point, then we have a certain flow. Then, if I can move them all the way in, we have a higher flow because we've gotten deeper in God. If the Bible says that inside of my body is the Spirit of God and me, and if it says that He searches the deep things of God, then when I have a problem, I come to Him and say, "Here's my problem and here's what I'm dealing with." He will give me an answer for as far as I can go, but if He's able to search the deep things of God, then He's able to go all the way. He's able to search the deep things, and then come back with the highest flow possible. If we understand that the Spirit of God searches the deep things of God, if you are very fleshly you'll stand at the door. You might receive a piece of the answer.

This is why people struggle with healing. They're comparing natural things with spiritual things. The Holy Ghost has already gone in, come back and said, "Look, you're healed. Father said to tell you you're healed." *Then why do I keep coughing? Why do I keep feeling this pain? I know, but why do I keep...you don't* *understand, this is...*Then you wonder why God doesn't speak to you. It's coming up to light. When I come up to light, I understand that whatever God is saying, I'm walking in. So when the Spirit of God goes in to search the deep things, so am I.

When I want answers, I'm not going to call my home girls. I'm about to send a knee-mail. You know what a knee-mail is? I'm going to get down on my knees and speak to God. I will wrestle with God. I'm not getting up out of this position until I receive an answer because I need to search the deep things of God. I don't want a superficial answer. I need a deep answer. I need an answer that moves all heaven and shakes hell. I need an answer that will resolve my situation. When I'm up against the wall I'm not playing. This isn't Tiddly Winks; I need real answers. That's why He said the Spirit searches the deep things. I don't know about you, but I'm tired of having a superficial God and blaming Him, as if that's Him, when He's like, "Come deeper. If you just come a little deeper."

There's a process by which God strips and break things off of you. As He breaks pieces off of you, you become a little lighter and start moving a little faster. As you go up, you start going into places of light where you have greater revelation and understanding than other people. Of course they become jealous, but if that's what it takes to walk in a deeper revelation, all I want is more God. I don't need more money, I need more anointing. I don't need more power, I need more God. I don't need more stuff, I need more revelation. I need more light.

We're not comparing spiritual and natural things because what I do by the Spirit may not make sense in the natural. For the most part, whatever God is going to ask you to do, it will not make sense in the natural. What happens in the realm of the Spirit is not about what happens in the natural and if you compare natural things with spiritual things, you'll miss out. Who would have thought that now, today, Rhema has Bible Training Centers in 80 countries around the world, all starting out with a dime. You can't even buy a candy bar for a nickel nowadays. I'd be as big as a wagon wheel if you could.

It's the Spirit that searches the deep things of God. You keep trying to find an answer in the natural. The problem is the natural is what created the question. Einstein said that problems can never be solved at the level of awareness that created it. If you want to be promoted in your job, you'd better know how to answer questions that are above your pay grade. If you can't solve a problem above your pay grade, then you will stay where you are. Promotion always comes when people recognize you can handle more than what you currently do. If you're freaking out with what you already have, then you don't qualify for promotion. Most people think that their promotion should be because they skillfully handle what they have. That's not when promotion comes. Promotion does not come because you can handle what you have. Promotion comes when you can handle more than what you have. If you understand the levels in God, then you understand when He said that the light shineth brighter and brighter unto a perfect day, He wants to take you from this place to this place. As you continue to grow and walk in more light, you may falter back a little bit but you'll step forward.

As you progress, you walk in greater degrees of light. The greater degree of light that you walk in, the greater success you will experience. However, you can't do it trying to hold on to the world, the stuff, and to yourself. When do you die to yourself? Natural things don't line up with spiritual things. Could you imagine if in our day Jesus healed a blind man the same way He did in the book of John? You have people that are so smart nowadays. *Well, if they're blind we're going to have to find some ocular implants and that's going to six thousand dollars per eye surgery. We're going to have to find the best surgeons in the planet. They're going to need some medication, we're going to have to prescribe this and that because that's the only way it's going to work.* Then Jesus walks up and spits on him. No $6,000 an eye, no medication. I'm trying to teach you to understand the supernatural ability of our God. He is not playing. This is real for Him. He doesn't subscribe to all of the natural rules. He can give you one word and it'll change your whole situation. He can give you one answer that'll change your whole life. All you have to do is recognize that you can't hear if you're not there.

You're trying to solve kiddy problems but God said you've grown up. You've got bigger issues, bigger fish to fry. *Yeah, but I'm still struggling with this addiction.* God's like, "Can we move past that? I need you to help other people break their addictions." *I'm still struggling with paying my bills.* Can we move past that? I want you to start paying other people's bills. *If You're going to bless me, God, then how come I don't have it?* You weren't walking by faith because faith says I have it before I see it. He calls it mine before I know it's there because faith is what I call those things that are not and so they are. That's faith. I don't care if I'm pushing a Hoopty; in my head it's a Bentley. *It sure don't look like no Bentley.* That's because you don't have eyes.

You have to understand the heart in which I'm sharing this with you because what I'm trying to tell you is that most things concerning God never line up with natural things. I've never in my life seen such spiritual attacks in different people as I have recently. If you're not being criticized or talked about, the Bible says be wary when everyone speaks well of you (Luke 6:26). In other words, if nobody has anything bad to say about you, you aren't doing it right.

When you watch the attack that people have gone through, you see that it's natural. It's but a light affliction as the apostle Paul called it. We have to learn that spiritual things are to be compared only to spiritual things. When I hear that God will supply all my need according to His riches in Christ Jesus (see Philippians 4:19), I don't gauge whether He supplied my need based on my natural understanding. I gauge only on what the Word says. People will take what God says and compare it to what is naturally going on. *"I don't feel like a conqueror. I'm getting whooped all of the time. I know God said He's going to prosper me and I know He'll heal me, but I haven't seen that yet."* That's natural. Real faith comes when you are able to unhook yourself from natural and allow your faith to be resonant in one thing: Did the Word say it?

Instead of me saying, "Am I healed? Let me see; do I feel healed? No, I don't feel healed," I go to my Bible and say, "Does God say I'm healed? Yes, He does. He says it here, and here, and here. So, then I must be." If I'm walking in light—because light comes as the Word comes—then there is no darkness. That's why the Bible says that darkness comprehended it not. A better word would have been "apprehended." Darkness cannot capture light, so the reason we struggle is because we don't take the Word at faith value. We want to compare it to natural things.

You can solve natural problems through spiritual means, but you can never solve a spiritual problem through natural means. Sometimes it takes the anointing to break that yoke. You can't think your way out of it, buy your way out, spend your way out, or feel your way out. You have to get to a place where you are walking by faith.

COMING UP TO LIGHT

When you walk by faith and not by sight, then you don't compare natural things anymore because you're not even looking. You're walking by faith. I've had people say, *"Pastor, I don't understand how sometimes you get in a situation and you just kind of know."* I couldn't even articulate to you how I know either, but I know. People have sat on the couch in my office and I start reading their mail like I was home with them. I wasn't, I promise you. Sometimes you live a life where you become so sensitive that you pick up stuff that nobody else picks up. That doesn't come because you're trying to be fleshly all the time. That doesn't come when you're all about natural things. If you want to search the deep things of God, then you'd better learn how to walk in light. As light comes, you qualify for more.

Light is an amazing thing. What happens is God will step in and it's like a puppet show that kids are enamored by. They don't know there's somebody's hand in the puppet, but we sit back and we know. Do you ever stop and think that God knows? The things you see and are enamored with, Satan's hand is in the puppet. God's looking at it and saying, "Hold on. Let me pull back the veil a little bit. Let me show you that he might be in church, she might be on the praise team, but let me pull back the veil just a little bit." The job you keep going after and want so desperately may be Satan's hand in the puppet. *"Well, my kids are acting up. I don't understand what's going on with my child."* God's saying, "If you would seek Me, if you would do some of the things I'm asking you to do, you would have greater light and understanding. Then I could pull back the veil and show you some things."

I remember Juanita Bynum telling a story about her sister who was strung out on drugs. Her nephew, her sister's son, ended up in a hospital bed and was dying. When her sister got news that her son was in the hospital dying, she came to my friend's house and said, "I just want to take a bath." She took a bath, got cleaned up, went down to the hospital, crawled up underneath the hospital bed where her son lie above her, and began to call and rebuke the demonic spirit out of his body—and he lived. I'm talking about that type of power! She might not have been living right, but she had enough sense to come up to light, to put herself under that bed, and call that sickness out of his body. I'm not talking about this pansy Christianity; I'm talking about real stuff. When's the last time you crawled up under a hospital bed and called that sickness out of a body? I'm talking about the deep things. I don't know about you. If superficial is enough for you, more power to you, but I want the deep things.

The apostle Paul said, "There are things I want to tell you but I can't even tell you. You're too carnal" (see 1 Corinthians 3:1). I want to be in a place where God trusts me enough to call me up, talk to me, and show me things He hasn't shown anyone else. I'm talking about deep things. I'm not talking about the normal revelation you have where you're like, *"Oh, God revealed some things to me."* Oh? What did He reveal to you? *"He made the birds and the trees."* That's good, but I passed that years ago. I need some deep things. I want to understand His ways. I want to be able to walk in His power. I want to be at a place like where Kathryn Kuhlman walked out of the airport and people fell out under the power of God. They thought a bomb went off because people fell out just because she was there. Can you imagine what would happen in this world if just your very presence convicted people? Do you have any idea what would happen if the God in you, the light you're walking in, was set at such a place that you could just sit down next to somebody and the power of God would convict? All of a sudden they would just repent and seek what is in you. I don't know about you, but I want that. I have been disrespected by the best. I've been cussed out by the best. I've been hung up on by the best. I don't care as long as He doesn't hang up on me...

Now I understand when people say, *"You have to work on your love walk."* You know what will help you walk in your love walk? Pastoring. When everything in you wants to smack and choke and all that comes out of you is, "God bless you." The words leave your mouth like they're not even yours. You're looking down like, "That's not what I was thinking." My brain sent a very different message to my mouth, but the love of God constrains me. I'm thinking, "You so-and-so!" and all that comes out is "God loves you and so do I." Really? You learn how to walk in light. You learn that your love walk is important. You can't have ill towards people and still prosper in God. I don't care what you think, you cannot hate your brothers and sisters in Christ and still walk in the power of God.

The Bible says he who hates his brother is a murderer and there's no light in him (1 John 2:9; 3:15). Light will cause you to love those that hate you. Light will cause you to love those that despitefully use you. You know what "despitefully uses you" means? When those people come in, you help them get their life back together, then they leave. You're just not a good pastor but you fixed their life for them. Perhaps their life falls apart and they come back. Then God uses you to help fix them up again, but they get bent out of shape over something you said or did. You became too close to them personally, you preached a message and stepped on their toes, then they're gone again.

You learn through those processes. You love them anyway. Why? You just have to. I have multiple companies, prosperity, and success. I cannot afford to walk around mad. I have people who are employed, people who gain from what I do. I don't have the luxury to be angry. There's too much riding on it. Although I may want to say thus and so, instead I say, "Hey, I love you. Did I ever tell you how pretty your eyes are? Come on over and give me a hug." If you don't love your brothers and sisters, you'll never prosper. If you don't love God, you'll never prosper.

Some people are playing church. You're doing it because you think this is what you're supposed to do. You're doing it because you're hedging your bet. *"If God is real, I'm covered. If God ain't real, I haven't put too much in it."* I hope, if anything, this message has helped you to understand that you're going to have to go a little bit deeper and walk in some light. When you hear the word preached, you know it's God, and it's pricking your heart, it's time to act on it. You don't try to figure out what it is— heartburn, indigestion, or maybe acid reflux. No, it's God and He's knocking. He's saying, "If you would only... all I need is... come on, just.... one more...." Line upon line. When you stop resisting and surrender, He has free rein. Then perhaps you will hit that season where it seems like nothing is happening, nothing seems to matter. But once you get there, welcome to the club. You've arrived. The very thing you've tried to avoid and are afraid of is the very thing that caused you to arrive.

GIVING ENTRANCE TO LIGHT

"The entrance of thy words giveth light; it giveth understanding unto the simple."
—*Psalms 119:130*

The Word does not give light; the Word *is* light. I could go into the middle of the mall and say something to the effect of "I am healed by the blood of Jesus." Is that light? Yes, but it doesn't mean anything or give light to anyone that doesn't know. So many people think that it's just the Word that gives light, but it's not the Word that gives light. It's the entrance of the Word that gives light. It's the opening and unfolding of the Word. You have the ability to deny light, to stay in ignorance and not have light. Not because God doesn't desire for you to have it, but because you can be so stubborn in certain areas of your life that you will not allow entrance. Like a dog with a wound. *"You can talk to me about money. I'm okay with that because I understand prosperity. You can talk to me about relationships because I can get clear with a relationship, but don't talk to me about healing. I've been sick for too long."* Or, *"I know how to get healed, I know how to walk in prosperity, but don't talk about my relationships because I'll date who I want to date and see who I want to see."*

I've watched people who God told not to get into a relationship with certain people, but they did it anyway and got sick. They don't even recognize the connection. Next thing you know their money's funny. It's the entrance that gives light. It's very simple. If I had a door and said, "Come on in to my house," but as soon as you take a step, I slammed the door. Wow, you're sitting on the outside and you have no entrance. I don't care how bright you shine, you have no entrance into my life. When the Bible says that it gives understanding to the simple, what it's saying to you is you can't go above the Word of God because it is the ultimate light. So if light is the Word and the Word is light, then if you want light, you have to permit its entrance.

When it comes in with entrance, it doesn't just come in and say, "Here I am!" It will unfold. You can read the same scripture 10 times and on the 11th time say, *"Oh my God, I never saw that before!"* The entrance brings light because you are a person who welcomes it. You say, *"I may not get it, but I want it. I may not understand it, but I need it."* Entrance, the unfolding, some translations say the opening of the Word, where it unfolds into your heart. You realize the Word is true. The Word is the only truth that actually withstands.

I've seen so many people reject light. When you tell them what the Word of God says about a particular matter, they don't care. *"I'll date the unbeliever. I'll even marry the unbeliever."* Then they come into my office and ask me to pray for their marriage. What do you want me to do? Do you want me to override God and you think I'm stupid enough to try? The entrance of the Word gives light. I remember one time my pastor's kid had a bag of chips and I asked her if I could have one. She said, "Yeah, you can have one." She held the bottom of the bag, and as I went to reach in there, I realized she meant I could have *one*. I can't even get to one.

Do you ever think that when you ask God to give you an answer, instead of getting out of the way allowing it to come in, you stand in the doorway and see if it'll get around you? The problem is that you're blocking and keeping the Word from

126

actually having first place and entrance into your life. You block it by your fears, because it's the way it's always been done, it's the way you've believed it all your life. When the entrance comes in, it unfolds, manifests, duplicates, replicates, and expands into your life. It explodes into your heart and all of a sudden you're like, "Whoa! This is just too much. I've got to sit down." I'm not eating until I get full, I'm eating until I get tired. I'm about ready to pass out.

I have to be careful because a lot of times when I study, I can go so deep into one thing that I'll become lost. Then I'll forget where I was going in the first place. I have to throw it into reverse, write it down, and come back to it later. When the Word is handled correctly, it has entrance into your life. It becomes real and unfolds. I've watched so many people think they are of some private interpretation. It's like, first thing you have to do as a believer is make a decision: Is the Word of God first in your life? Are you going to allow it to have entrance?

For example, the way we settle arguments (I know it's hard to believe we have arguments but we do. We have spirited debate. We can disagree without being disagreeable) is by going to the Word. That takes both of us out of being right or wrong. When the Word has entrance into marriage, then the marriage has to be successful. When the Word has entrance into my heart, my heart has to be successful. When the Word has entrance into my physical body, then my physical body has to be successful. If there is light in the Word and I want to walk in greater light, then I have to walk in the greater understanding of the Word. I don't need more money, I don't need a better job, I don't need more stuff. What I need is more light. I need more understanding. In all my getting, I will get understanding. After I pursue after light, then I have to allow the entrance of those words to come in so it gives me light. As it gives me light, it makes me smart, brilliant, a genius, the smartest kid in the room. Light gives understanding unto simple folks.

The problem is if you're pretty high-minded of yourself, then you think you don't need light because you have it all figured out. That's why you live in hell. You might be saved, so you'll get to heaven, but you're living in hell now. I'm simple. I welcome the Word. People will say, *"Pastor, I'm struggling with my finances."* Well, okay. Let's talk about that. *"I know the Bible says..."* You haven't given entrance. Whatever you give entrance to, you will give utterance. *"I don't know what's wrong. Everything in my life is upside down."* You're giving utterance to that which has entered. What has entered is now what you are uttering. Utterance is equal to your entrance. You can allow fear entrance and what you will utter is fear. Fear gives darkness. So we wonder, "How do we walk in greater degrees of light?" It's the entrance of light.

A lot of times people's coping mechanisms are to deal with things in dysfunctional ways. If a person suffers from abandonment issues, they don't like being left alone and can't be by themselves. Because of that, they have learned to act like a wounded dog. Over time, when this happens, everyone comes running. They've learned that if they act like a wounded dog, they will get the attention that they so crave and that they could not get by just telling somebody, "Hey, I want your attention." So now because this is a coping mechanism, 25 years later, they're still that one who can't seem to cope with situations and circumstances because they've learned if they do this, then they get that.

Now here's the problem, however; everybody around them can't stand them. The only people who come to their aid are people who enjoy seeing them hurt. If you can't come to my rescue and bring me out of it, you are not there for me, you are there for you.

Anybody who comes to my rescue must come with the understanding that I came to get you out of this situation. I love you too much to leave you right there. I'm not there to commiserate with you. I'm not there to cry with you. I might cry for a little while, but we're going to suck up those tears and square off our shoulders. We're coming out of this thing. However, when people just want to see you hurt, they don't care about you coming out.

People who have coping mechanisms are unhealthy. They use this coping mechanism so much, so many times, and so often that now they get actually derive satisfaction— not out of your attention anymore but out of the actual act of moping. Now every time something goes wrong, that's what they do. They literally make themselves feel better because they're certain that if they do that, they'll feel a certain way. Every time you leave the house, the dog chews your slippers. Five minutes later, the dog has no recollection. They don't chew the slippers to get you to come home. They do at the time, but five minutes later it has no recollection that it chewed the slippers to make any connection to you coming home to the slippers, but it does it anyway because it gets pleasure out of chewing your slippers. You have to be careful because once you allow entrance, now all of a sudden this becomes a lifestyle. That which you allow to enter in, now you're wrestling with the devil trying to change it. Whatever has entrance is utterance. Whatever you allow in comes out.

Remember, Jesus said it's not what goes in the man's mouth that defiles him, it's what comes out of it (Matthew 15:11). Isn't that something? What do you give entrance to? What do you allow into your life? What is it that you continually give utterance to? Whatever you give utterance to is what you have given entrance to. If you are constantly uttering the word, then you have given entrance. If you are constantly uttering your problem... Some people, I don't even want to ask you how you're doing. I can see the mope. It's so demonic. People think that the Word gives light. The Word does not give light, the entrance of it does. That's why the Bible says faith cometh by hearing and hearing by the word of God (Romans 10:17).

"I heard this all before, Pastor." I don't care because the moment you say you've heard it all before, I can tell by your utterance you gave no entrance. I can hear the same word preached over and over and over again and every single time I will get something new. I've had people walk up to me and say, *"Pastor, that was one of the best messages I've ever heard."* Here's what I'm thinking: "You've been here for two to three years; I've taught this six times. All I did was repackage it. You mean to tell me you never heard none of this before?" I've learned that repetition is the mother of all skill. I know that people only retain 20 percent of what you say. What I try to do is make 20 percent all 100 percent so that way when you've heard 100 percent of it, even if you only catch 20 percent that's pretty much all I said anyway.

What gives light is not the Word itself. Faith cometh by hearing and hearing by the Word of God. It does not come by only hearing once. I have to hear it over and over and over again. Why? Because I probably didn't give entrance to it the first time. I might not even have known it was knocking. That's why a word in season knocks on the door of my heart because of what I'm going through at that precise moment. When I hear the knock and open the door I'm like, "Whoa! Problem, meet answer." When that moment happens I have what is called an epiphany. I'm like, "Oh my God, that's the answer! Where have you been all my life?" Now light has come and it gives understanding to the simple because now I get it. Faith cometh by hearing, hearing by the Word of God.

"Thy word is a lamp unto my feet and a light unto my path."
—*Psalm 119:105*

I carry a lamp unto my feet so I can see where my feet are going, and so I don't stumble and possibly fall. A light unto my path illuminates my directions. The reason people stumble is that they don't have direction. One of the most popular statements said to me is, *"If I knew what God wanted me to do, I would do it."* The Bible is God telling you. *"Well, I'm not reading all of that. Don't they have some Cliff Notes?"* Yeah, it's called the Holy Ghost. You ever met Him? The Word is a lamp unto your feet to keep you from stumbling and it's a light unto your path to direct you. The problem is because people don't value the Word of God. Some people don't even crack their Bible until they come to church and they barely do it in church because the words are on the screen. I know pastors who refuse to put Scripture on the screen, saying, "If you don't have a Bible, you'll just have to deal with it until you get one." If I want direction in my life, then I must have the Word, because the Word of God gives me direction and keeps me from stumbling.

It's like dating an unbeliever and being unequally yoked. Unequally yoked doesn't just mean being with an unbeliever. If you have a call of God on your life, you better make sure the person you're with has a commensurate call. If you're not commensurate in your call, equal on your call (not equal on the level or equal in purpose), you will face struggle after struggle. It'll be like trying to jam a square peg into a round hole. It just doesn't fit.

Do you have any idea how many people don't grasp that and then they wonder why they're tripping and stumbling, trying to find direction. They're using external circumstances to create direction. *"Well, I'm lonely."* So what? Buy a puppy; it's cheaper in the long run. If you get mad, they'll still lick your face. They're good to you. (Don't get a cat. Dogs have owners and cats have staff.) So, because these folks won't allow the Word to be a lamp unto their feet, they stumble. Nothing destroys a call faster than a person hooking up with the wrong person, not to mention the idea of dating an unbeliever. The Bible asks what fellowship light has with darkness. What do you discuss? *"We just talk about worldly stuff."* Then I have to ask are *you* even saved? Maybe you're *not* unequally yoked.

When light comes, it's a lamp for me. It illuminates the pitfalls—the rocks, the stubble and the bushes, the things I need to see. It directs my path because it's a light unto my path and it shows me which way to go. When the Word comes into my life, I give it first place. Even if my feelings are involved, I have to let whatever it is go. Not because of you, but because the Word is clear to me that this is not going to work. I wish it would, but it's not going to because it's not in line with the Word. There's nothing worse than someone who refuses to understand what is on their life in terms of God. When they're running from God, you have to be careful. Light should have come. At what point does God keep trying to bring light into a person's life and they keep shutting it down, rejecting it, so what they will not give entrance to eventually will choke? So many people don't walk in light. They reject it and will not give entrance to the Word. When you deal with them, what else do we have?

"This know also, that in the last days perilous times shall come. For men shall be lovers of their own selves, covetous, boasters, proud, blasphemers, disobedient to parents, unthankful, unholy, without natural affection, truce breakers, false accusers, incontinent, fierce, despisers of those that are

good, traitors, heady, high-minded, lovers of pleasure more than lovers of God, having a form of godliness but denying the power of it; from such turn away. For of this sort are they who creep into houses, and lead captive silly women laden with sins, led away with divers lusts, ever learning, and never able to come to the knowledge of the truth."
—*2 Timothy 3:1-7*

Ever learning, constantly in the Word, but never able to come to the knowledge of truth. They're silly. Let's move past the gender aspect of it and into the understanding of trying to learn. Ever learning, but never coming to the knowledge. Light is knocking, light is present. When they are trying to learn, are they around light? Yes. Are they possibly even seeing light? Yes. Is the light given entrance? No. Therefore, there's no knowledge of the truth. I know people who can spit scripture to you, but they have no understanding of it because they have no light. They get the context, the actual words themselves, but they have no Holy Spirit revelation.

I don't care how much of the Word you know. It's not about what you know, it's about what's in you. "Beloved, I wish above all things that thou mayest prosper and be in health, even as thy soul prospereth" (3 John 1:2). Your soul is your mind, will, and emotions. Your mind has to become fruitful. You cannot prosper beyond what you have revelation of. If your revelation is that you can't afford to give, you've given utterance to that which you've given entrance to. Now because you've given utterance, you're right. You'll never be able to afford to give. This is the place where people are ever learning. You have to be careful with people who tell you they don't need to go to church because they sit at home and God speaks to them directly. The devil is a liar.

"Knowing that shortly I must put off this my tabernacle, even as our Lord Jesus Christ hath shown me. Moreover, I will endeavor that ye may be able, after my decease, to have these things always in remembrance. For we have not followed cunningly devised fables when we made known unto you the power and coming of our Lord Jesus Christ, but were eyewitnesses of his majesty. For he received from God the Father, honor and glory, when there came such a voice to him from the excellent glory, This is my beloved Son, in whom I am well pleased. And this voice which came from heaven we heard, when we were with him in the holy mount. We have also a more sure word of prophecy, which ye do well that ye take heed, as unto a light that shineth in a dark place, until the day dawn, and the day star arise in your hearts; Knowing this first, that no prophecy of the scripture is of any private interpretation. For the prophecy came not in old time by the will of man, but holy men of God spoke as they were moved by the Holy Ghost."
—2 Peter 1:14-21

Peter is explaining that he was there on the Mount of Transfiguration and saw God open up the heavens. He heard it with his own ears. He was present at the time where God Himself spoke, but he said we have a more sure word of prophecy. Nothing God will ever say will contradict that which He already said. This is why it's so important to be taught, trained, and developed. You can go off believing what Mama and others said but we have a more sure word. You can go off believing what you thought you heard God say to you, but we have a more sure word. What more sure word is Peter talking about? The Word of God. He said you would do well to take heed to it. To take heed to it means to hear and obey. I know this is what it's supposed to be so I'm going to be obedient to it. I'll be willing and obedient and I'll eat the good of the land. People don't eat the good of the land because they're not willing and obedient. *God, if You tell me to do it, I'll do it. If I'm supposed to surrender my life, I'll surrender. If I'm supposed to give it to You, I'll give it.* I've watched so many people with great calls on their life throw their call down the drain and suffer through the process. Some people cannot say no. It's a fire shut up in my bones. I can't, I won't, I refuse, I'll die first.

You would do well to take heed. Take heed as if it's a light that shines in a dark place because the entrance of the Word gives light and you need light if you're in a dark place. It says until the day dawn and the day star rises in your hearts, until your full light comes, until the situation is resolved. What do you do until you know that full revelation has come? Take heed to the Word. How do I know she's the right one for me? Take heed to the Word until light comes. How do I know that I'm going to prosper? Take heed to the Word. What does the Word say? "Give, and it shall be given unto you;...pressed down, and shaken together, and running over, shall men give into your bosom. For with the same measure that ye measure, it shall be measured to you again" (Luke 6:38). Take heed, hear and obey the word, until full light comes. If you want revelation before you obey, you might as well lock yourself in a class with doubting Thomas. The very essence of your faith is to act based on your faith, not based on you being convinced.

> *"Knowing this first, that no prophecy of the scripture is of any private interpretation. For the prophecy did not come by the will of man, but holy men of God spoke as they were moved by the Holy Ghost."*
> *— 2 Peter 1:20-21*

I got some new theology. God told me some things about this scripture that nobody knows. There are no private interpretations, they're public. What God has in the scriptures is not private, it's public. What was written in scripture was not because man willed it to be written. The Greek word for "moved" is the same word for wind in the sail of a sail boat. In other words, holy men of God were blown on by God Himself. They were moved, impelled, and directed by the wind of God. The breath of God moved people to write what they wrote. He said, "We have a more sure word which is that which is written." That which is written trumps that which I heard.

Even though I had a miraculous experience with God, I felt the power of God and He touched me in ways that no one could ever touch me before, I saw Jesus transfigured right before my eyes and had this supernatural experience, we have a more sure word. Some of you are looking for light to come in supernatural ways and because you are focused on what appears to be spectacular, you have missed the supernatural. You haven't given entrance because you're waiting for light to kick your door down.

It is the engrafted Word that is able to save your soul. Someone may suffer a serious burn on their skin so doctors will do a graft. They'll take skin from one spot, put it on another, and see if the body accepts or rejects it. If the body accepts it, then the skin has been successfully grafted. If it's the engrafted Word that is able to save my soul, then it's only the Word that I allow to be placed upon the sores and the ills and the weaknesses, sicknesses, problems, and challenges of my life. If I take the Word, apply it to those areas and accept it, then now it's able to save my soul. When light comes, what do you do with it?

Some pastors are afraid to talk about certain subjects, things on the underhanded side, that they don't want to draw light to. One of the reasons I'm able to talk about certain things is because I couldn't care less. It is what it is, that's why I don't have fear about it. I don't care if everybody gets offended and leaves. God will bring more people. I don't want fugitives, God will bring the right people. I trust Him and not you. However, the fact of the matter is if you won't honor Him in your finances, you will never prosper. Light has come, and if you don't give entrance to that light, then you're operating in darkness. The Bible says how great is darkness that can overcome light.

We have light, the Word comes; we have a problem, we seek the Word. What does the Word say about the matter? The Word says this, this, and this. Now, what am I going to do? Now I'm faced with a choice. Do I do what the Word says? How do I know when I'm not in faith? When there's a presence of doubt. How does doubt come? *"Well, I'm not sure God's going to do it this time. I know God healed other people but I don't know if He's going to heal me."* That's doubt. Faith is not only knowing that God can, but He will. The devil knows that God can. The sad part is the devil knows that God already has. It's you who struggles with faith. When you get into real faith, if you want real faith, then light has to come. When real faith is present, so is light. Now when people say to me, *"Well, Pastor, I'm struggling with my faith."* You're not struggling with faith, you're struggling with light and giving entrance. If you would give entrance to the light, then in itself the light would produce faith.

The Bible says that not all men have faith. Thessalonians tells us that we have been "delivered from unreasonable and wicked men; for not all men have faith" (2 Thessalonians 3:2). The Bible also tells us that God has dealt a measure of faith to every man. How do we qualify that? It's the God-type of faith. That's why the Bible says not every man has faith. I have been delivered from wicked and unreasonable men because not all men have God-type faith. When I show up in a place and people are dealing with me in an unreasonably and wicked way, it's because they don't have the God-type of faith. However, I thank God my miracles are not dependent upon their faith. They can have demonic faith all they want but when I show up in the house, every demon in hell has to know that I have faith. That's why I thank God that I'm delivered from unreasonable and wicked men. I say that all the time, I don't care what the situation is.

Not all men have faith, but I do. The Bible says I've been dealt a measure of faith. So now, my measure can be increased. To one Jesus said, "How is it you have so little faith?" (Matthew 8:26). Then He said to the centurion, "How do you have such great faith? I've not seen such great faith in all of Israel" (Matthew 8:5-10). That means that some people can have little faith, some can have great faith, and some can have no faith. If everyone can have different levels of faith, that means that if I want to grow in my faith, I have to give entrance to light.

If I want to grow my faith, then I have to give greater entrance. When I give greater entrance, when I'm studying my Bible at home first thing in the morning, when I'm consuming enough Word, when I'm attending a church, showing up every time I can, when the doors are open and I'm there to get fed, I'm literally consuming more and more light. More and more revelation is coming. Now I'm moving into that place of becoming a spiritual giant because as I grow and light comes and I give entrance to it, I don't tell God, "You can talk to me about this, but You can't talk to me about that." Here's the truth: If you are not good with your money, you will not be good with your healing. If you're not good with your healing, you will not be good with other areas of your life and you will face a full-blown attack. I've known people who literally, because they're stubborn about their money, are attacked in their body. *"I ain't feeling it. "* That doesn't affect me, for all men have not faith. I've been delivered.

Many of you are going through an attack and you're in transition. When people are in transition, they're transitioning to the next level. So many of us are in that transition place where it's just uncomfortable, but to be on this level requires greater faith. To get greater faith, I have to give greater entrance, I have to walk in greater light. If I try to just have more faith, it doesn't work. What I'm hoping is that the Word gives light. What I'm focused on now is the Word giving me light without me giving it entrance. If I give entrance, I open the door to you. I invite you in. I have a table set, we sit down together, and we have dinner. Entrance means that I'm bringing you in on purpose.

Not that I expect you from the outside of the door to bust my door down and force me to eat with you. That's called hostile takeover, but people expect that. What they don't understand is if you want to grow in greater faith, you're going to have to say, "God, let me give You greater entrance. You know that area I didn't want You to touch? It's Yours." Medically speaking, if you have a wound that hasn't been dealt with, it'll get infected. And if you go to the hospital or doctor, they have to dig it out, medicate it, and then treat it because you can't let it continue to fester.

If we don't give entrance in certain areas of our lives, it festers. Then when God wants to deal with it, as soon as He touches it, you retreat. He knows it hurts, but if you had not kept it in the dark and hid it from Him for so long it wouldn't hurt so much. You growled at him every time He went anywhere near it.

When your pastor taught on healing, you rolled your eyes. When he taught on money, you complained that's all he talked about. That's how you know you are not listening and I struck a chord because now it becomes amplified. *"All Pastor talks about is serving God."* You're in the church. What else am I supposed to talk about? Should we talk about some tires? Serving God, loving God, giving to God, supporting God, doing God.

These are ways you know that I've struck a chord. Offense is always the meter of what you don't want to deal with. I've seen people in relationships just because they're afraid of being alone. My dad would say they're like buses: If you wait around long enough, another one will come rolling by. We're not going to get yoked up because we're lonely. If you can't be alone, that means you don't like yourself. The only person who's going to like you is somebody who doesn't like you either. You teach people how to treat you. Light just came. This is how light comes, I give light entrance.

Any area that God wants to talk to me about? Come on in, let's sit awhile. Let's have some tea and crumpets. Let's let this marinate for a minute. What do You want me to do, God? How do You want me to handle this? Where do You want me to go? What does the Word say? I'll do the Word until light comes. Faith cometh by hearing and hearing by the Word of God. Notice it doesn't say faith is released by hearing. Faith is released by doing.

Some people struggle with their love walk. They struggle with loving their brothers and sisters. If you can't love your brothers and sisters in Christ, who do you love? The world? If you don't love the world, what's left? People wonder why they're struggling and it makes no sense. We have to give entrance to the Word in our lives. We have to make a point to say, "God, any part of my life that You want to have access to, You can have it. Anything that You want to speak to me, I want to hear it. If I'm a little offended by certain things, if there are subjects that are a little touchy to me, that's the area where I need to get out of the doorway and let it come on in. That's what's holding me back, blocking my blessings and keeping me from getting to the next level."

When you give entrance, that's when He said, "Thy word is a lamp unto my feet, and a light unto my path" (Psalm 119:105). It helps me to see so I don't stumble, and it gives me my direction. How easy is life when I have direction? How easy is life when I'm not stumbling? Some people stumble their way through life. It's painful and it hurts. We miss opportunities because we're stumbling our way through it. It's time to no longer stumble. I don't know what it's going to take for you, but to me it means to be circumspect and say, "Okay God, what areas of my life have I not given entrance to?" If you want to know what areas you haven't given entrance to, check what you've given utterance to. Whatever you've given utterance to, that's what you've given entrance to.

JUDGING LIGHT CORRECTLY

There's a difference between what people say and what people do. If you want to judge an individual, you don't judge them by what they say, you judge them by what they do. We are allowed to be fruit inspectors. In other words, we can judge fruit. This would help many of you in your relationships and your decisions about who you are going to invest time into—whether it be from a mentor, friendship, boyfriend or girlfriend, or from a marriage standpoint. Whatever you're going to invest your life into, you ought to look for some fruit. I've seen many people who ignore fruit and only look for what people say. The problem is, if I keep saying something over and over to you, faith cometh by hearing and hearing by the Word of God. I would not have to specify the Word of God if the God-type of faith came just by hearing. If it came just by hearing, then you could get faith by hearing anything. The Bible tells you to have the God-type of faith, then faith cometh by hearing and hearing by the Word of God. That means that repetitious things can cause us to believe.

You've seen it before in your life. That one girl who's so desperate to get that one guy that she eventually ends up with him because she wore him down. If he had an aversion to her from jump, there was a reason for that. However, faith cometh by hearing. That's why the Bible says to beware the temptress for her lips drip like honey (Proverbs 5:3). Watch out for that particular guy or girl because their words can be like warm honey in your ear. They know what to say and how to push the buttons. The way to avoid all of that is to look for fruit. You can fabricate fruit, but it won't taste very good. You will know it's plastic fruit after you spend some time investigating.

The challenge we have is that people don't often look for fruit, they look at superficial things. The Bible tells us if we say we have fellowship but we live in darkness, we walk out darkness, we do things in darkness, then we're lying because we do not the truth. The Bible is very clear to help us understand that we are expected to walk in light. I cannot tell you how many times I've brought light to a particular situation and people will then turn around and do the exact opposite. The challenge is they're expecting a different result than what the Bible says.

We have be circumspect in our lives. The Bible says, "If we walk in light...." "If" implies that there is a possibility we will not be walking in light. It implies that there's a choice that has to be made as to whether or not we walk in light. The Word of God does not bring light, the entrance of the word is what brings light—our willingness and obedience to receive and accept the Word as the final authority in our lives.

The Bible tells you to love. I don't care what they did to you; faith worketh by love. The word "worketh" means explosion, or energia. Our faith is energized by love. The very nature of what makes faith explosive is love. If you do not walk in love, your faith will not work. I don't know about you, but I require my faith. I know every one of you, your lives are perfect. You have all the things that you need, and everything you've ever wanted is all there so you don't know what I'm talking about. I'm talking about when you need your faith to produce and manifest to move a mountain. When you need your faith, faith worketh by love.

Biblical light is the foundation of faith. When light comes, faith comes. Faith is not released by hearing, but faith shows up. Now what happens when it's rejected? You have also rejected God. So if I come to your house and knock upon your door, I have come. If faith comes by hearing and hearing by the Word of God, then the entrance of the Word is what gives light. Then faith comes and faith and light are the same thing. When you refuse light, you refuse faith. This is why people struggle. They're wondering why things don't work for them. It's because they've denied the Word which means they've rejected light. Because they've rejected light, no faith is present. Faith came but they slammed the door.

"He that committeth sin is of the devil; for the devil sinneth from the beginning. For this purpose the Son of God was manifested, that he might destroy the works of the devil."
—1 John 3:8

The word "destroy" in the Greek means to unravel. If you have a piece of string from a fabric and you pull the string, the next thing you know that string gets longer. You unravel, or take apart, the very fabric or nature of something. The Bible said that the Son of God was made manifested that He might destroy, that He might completely unravel and take apart from the very seams the works of the devil. In the language we see here, it almost gives the thought process that if I make a mistake and I sin, then I'm of the devil. That's not what this is saying. The word "committeth" is probably better translated as "he who practices sin," one who has light, but chooses darkness. It's one thing to not know God, period. It's another to know and not do. When we know better, we are supposed to do better. James is saying that he who practices sin is of the devil because the only way you can love light more than darkness is you have to be of God. The only way you could practice sin, love it unto death, is you have to be of the devil as the devil sinneth from the beginning.

From the very beginning, from the onset, the devil was sinning. If you knew better, you would do better. Most people—when they first come into the things of God—they start cleaning up. It might take some longer than others but they start down that road. Then something happens, and depending on how you respond to that determines how you live from that point forward. Usually, if you have all knowledge about God, you knew you were created by Him personally, you were in His presence, it's hard to keep sinning from the beginning. It might be that I've been derailed for a period of time, but to say that the devil sinneth from the beginning, he's been wrong since jump and has refused. He's committed.

Can you imagine what this would have been like to be the covering angel, the angel of worship and the anointing, to be going up and down on the throne of God, to be in God's presence and lead angels in worship to God and to have that understanding and knowledge, and still be a sinner. I can get as mad as I want with Adam and Eve, but they were human beings. They were not angels, created beings in the anointing and in the covering of God in the heavens. They might have been stupid, but seriously?

I wish we could get Christians who are as sold out for God as Satan is sold out for sin. He never backs off. He doesn't say, "I think they've been through enough. All right guys, we hit them with cancer and they beat that so that's enough. Every good, decent human being deserves a break." No, because he practices sin. He's good at it, he's learned how to deceive. He's learned how to live in sin and act a fool and still show up for church.

146

You know how people say, "practice makes perfect"? That is not true. Perfect practice makes perfect, but whatever you practice, if you practice it wrong you will do it wrong. We know that what people do out in the field or on the court is a manifestation of how they practiced. Satan practices sin, and anyone who practices sin the way he does is of him. When you practice sin, you learned how to hide it. You've learned how to do it and not get caught. You've learned how to sell it and not let anybody know about it. You've learned how to do things without anybody ever being the wiser. You start to do things in the dark without anyone knowing.

James says for this very reason, the Son of God was manifested that he might destroy, unravel, tear into pieces, shred the works of the devil. When light comes, exposure comes. Your works will become revealed so that people can see what manner they are. This is where Jesus, as the light of the world, becomes so indwelled in us that we can no longer do what we used to do. It's imperative you understand that it is not about doing what you want to do.

> *"But God hath revealed them unto us by his Spirit; for the Spirit searcheth all things, yea, the deep things of God. For what man knoweth the things of a man, save the spirit of man which is in him? Even so the things of God knoweth no man but the Spirit of God. Now we have received, not the spirit of the world, but the Spirit who is of God; that we might know the things that are freely given to us of God. Which things also we speak; not in the words which man's wisdom teacheth, but which the Holy Ghost teacheth, comparing spiritual things with spiritual."*
> —*1 Corinthians 2:10-13*

"But if our gospel be hidden, it is hidden to them that are lost. In whom the god of this world hath blinded the minds of them who believe not, lest the light of the glorious gospel of Christ, who is the image of God, should shine unto them. For we preach not ourselves, but Christ Jesus the Lord, and ourselves your servants for Jesus' sake."
—2 Corinthians 4:3-5

Who knows the deep things of God except for the Spirit of God, and who knows the heart of a man like the spirit of man does? He's talking about the deep things concerning God, the deep cryeth out unto the deep. These are the rich things of God. These are the answers that never seem to come. These are the solutions that we never seem to get hold of. This is that healing we've been digging for and can't seem to get it to manifest. There are certain things that are the deep things of God. We want direction, to know where God wants us to go and what to do, and Paul said that in Christ you have access to the Holy Ghost. As the Holy Ghost speaks and teaches you things, He instructs you by bringing light. That's why 2 Corinthians says that the gospel be hid. They're blinded to the light by Satan himself, the god of this world. He's not the god of the world, he's the god of this world.

There is a world's system that is in operation and functioning right now even as we speak. This system is not created to be a benefit to you. It's not created to bless you; it's created to kill, steal, and destroy. It includes finances, your health, your prosperity, and your relationships. Look at how relationships have come under attack in the last 10-15 years. Marriage is not even something people consider nowadays. I've seen people date for five or six years and never have a discussion about marriage. The devil is a lie. "What's the reason? There's no benefit." It's the world's system.

God is not *in control of* everything that happens, God is *sovereign over* everything that happens. There's a difference. Sometimes people think, *"How come I keep going through this and that? What is God doing to me?"* God hasn't done anything to you. God is sovereign over all of it, which means none of it affects Him. However, there is a god of this world and he is not your friend nor is he your pal.

You ever hear people say, "I don't know that I can do the Christian thing, I've got to be free." The Bible talks about how you used to walk according to the course of this world. That means in the same way a rat is placed into a maze and follows a specific pattern to find cheese, that's the course. It's a predetermined path. While people proclaim to be free, they have no idea that whom the Son sets free is free indeed. They are living according to a course, a predetermined plan, that leads to nothing but death, destruction, and theft. They mix the God of the world with the god of this world. Then they think God is behind all of the things they're going through in their life. It's hid from them. Satan blinds them to keep them functioning in the course of this world where they value the job more than they do church, value stuff more than they do their spiritual family, and value a life coach more than they do a pastor. They'll pay the life coach $100 an hour, but they'll put $2 in the offering.

When you look at this, you will see that the course of the world has unfortunately crept into the church. Now the biggest church is the one with the best band and the smoke machine. *"Well, that was spectacular. Did you see that light show?"* I'd rather have people getting healed on this platform who limped up and walked off. I don't need a fog machine. When the power of God shows up, He brings His own fog. We should be learning to practice how to get in His presence. When we learn how to get into His presence, He shows up and shows out. This is what we have to know as believers because the rest of the world walks according to the course of the world.

Some of you Christians folks...you know how you all are. *"I don't understand. They just go drinking and partying all the time. What's wrong with them?"* The course of this world. *"I invite them and they just don't come!"* It's the course of this world, they're doing what they were created to do. Judas did what he was created to do. Pharaoh did what he was created to do. Can anyone come to light? Yes, but can you force them? No. It's the entrance of light. They've got to allow it in. People don't always allow the entrance of light. They struggle and come to me and say, "Pastor I'm struggling with something. Here's my problem," And I'll give them a biblical answer. Some will walk out of my office saying, "I'm so glad I went and talked to Pastor because I got an answer and a solution!" Others, however, will walk out and say, "I don't know why he just won't help me. Somehow I thought he'd just give me the answer." Two people, same answer, different results.

There's a course of this world and if you're not careful, you will go back to patterns that you learned when you were in this course. One of the biggest challenges to someone who's been clean and sober is stress. In stress they've learned by certainty to do something that creates an emotional state. They've learned if they get completely stressed out, they can go to the club and get drunk, completely blasted, and will not be concerned with anything that has happened until the next day. Whether or not they remember what happens, that helps them. While you may say, *"Oh, you don't remember what you did? That's terrible,"* in their head when they're trying to escape, that's great. Now they've learned through conditioning that they've created something they know is certain. *If*

I do this, then I get that. If I hit that pipe, I get this. If I smoke weed, I get this. There's a certainty that comes because now they know every time they get stressed, they can escape. Rats in the maze; conditioning.

When you understand there's a course in the world, you understand greater revelation when he said if our gospel be hid. The god of this world has blinded the minds of those who do not believe, lest the light of the glorious light of the gospel of God should shine unto them. The only way that a person who does not believe will not see the light of Christ is it has to be hid. The light is so bright that the only way you cannot see it is if there was a purposeful plan to keep you from shining. If it wasn't hid from them, they'd see it like we see it and they would understand it like we understand it. How great does darkness have to be to overcome light, because the presence of light is the absence of darkness. If to us who believe, if the gospel shines as light unto us, how great does darkness have to be for us? We are not among those who believe not, we're among those who believe. How great do you have to love your pet sin? How great do you have to desire it for it to overshadow the light that's in you? We know Satan has blinded those who don't believe, but what's your excuse? You're not blinded by Satan, or at least you shouldn't be.

Paul said for we preach not ourselves, but Christ Jesus our Lord and as servants for Jesus' sake. We're not telling you things that are of us; we are servants to you and servants to Christ. We are serving you because of Christ and the light we bring to you is because Christ is bringing it through us, the hope in you. This is where the rubber hits the road, where we are circumspect about our lives. We say, if there's a proper way to establish a relationship, to be in a marriage, to live my life, then do I act like a believer where light has shined so I can now shine light or am I as dark as the person next to me who is in the world? Am I as dark as the coworker who's so excited to drink and party at happy hour? Do I accept darkness because I have endured stress? Do I go back to my normal routines? This is what happens in the course of this world. As people are being pulled out of the world, they go to what's natural.

CHOOSING LIGHT OVER DARKNESS

"I have come a light into the world, so whosoever believeth on me should not abide in darkness."
— John 12:46

     Some translations say "should not" and others say "may not." It's still the same, but it doesn't say they *cannot.* You shouldn't but you could. "May not" is you may, or you may not. Therefore, it's telling you that Jesus said He came into the world as light so that whoever believes in Him has the potential, the possibility, to not remain in darkness. "If any man hear my words, and believe not, I judge him not; for I came not to judge the world but to save the world" (John 12:47).

     Here's what people do: They want to have what they deem to be a relationship with Jesus. *"I love Jesus so I'm saved."* You are saved because you accept Jesus. People think they're good Christians as long as they love Jesus. "The one who rejects me and does not receive my words has a judge. The word that I have spoken will judge him." Jesus said He didn't come to judge you; He's not interested in judging you. He has one mission—to save you. Here's the problem, however: You're not off the hook because He says you still have a judge—His Word. When people seek a relationship with Christ and they don't think it's important to have a relationship with His Word, they do not understand that they will be judged by the Word. So if you don't understand, the Word of the gospel is hidden from you. *"I don't know that it's important to go to church. Why do I need to go to church?"* To learn the Word. Why do you need to learn the Word? Because that's what you're going to be judged by. It's like having the test before you take it. That's what makes this whole thing an open book test.

What is the judge? The Word. We know that Jesus is the Word made flesh. Jesus is, in fact, the Word, yet He said, "As my earthly ministry, I am not here to judge you. I'm here to save you, in this form, as Jesus Christ. However, as Christ Jesus—deity, the one who is, was, and will always be—when I come back as the Lion of the Tribe of Judah, everyone who has rejected Me, I will judge. You will all stand before Me and you will give an account of what you've done in your body, whether good or bad. You will render an account for your life."

The question will be, how close have you come to the things that God has foreordained since the very foundations of the world? Do you understand that He gave you the Word as the answer book? He said He didn't come to judge now, but He came to save. Whoever rejects Him, His Word will judge them.

I've told people countless times, "Don't do this, and here are the reasons why. This is what the Word says about it." Light is coming, light has shown up, it has knocked on the door. Then they do the exact opposite of what I said. Now the same light that came to help has become their judge. I submit to you that if you think about it, there are plenty of times in your life where you knew what to do, but you did not do it and it judged you. You then dealt with the consequence—not because of you, but because of how you chose to handle it.

We have to be careful that we are not blinded. We have to see and discern light when it shows up. We have to be at a place where we understand what is light. When we have true light, we have to walk in it. Many people who have light on the subject go around and do the exact same thing, then wonder why their life is falling apart. It doesn't work that way. The light that was coming is now the same light that will judge.

> *"Therefore, whosoever heareth these sayings of mine and doeth them, I will liken him unto a wise man, who built his house upon a rock. And the rain descended, and the floods came, and the winds blew and beat upon that house, and it fell not, for it was founded upon a rock. And every one that heareth these sayings of mine, and doeth them not, shall be likened unto a foolish man, who built his house upon the sand. And the rain descended, and the floods came, and the winds blew and beat upon that house, and it fell, and great was the fall of it."*
> —Matthew 7:24-27

Did you notice that both the person they called wise who built his house upon the rock, heard it and did it, and the person who heard it and didn't do it, both went through the same attack. Sometimes we think that because we're Christians, the attack goes away. We think that God's deliverance comes because He takes away. He doesn't take away the attack, however, he unravels. The attack still comes, but when your house is built upon the rock, you can withstand and endure the attack because you heard the Word and you did the Word.

If you heard the Word on giving and you do the Word concerning your giving, then guess what? When Satan comes to attack your life, you have built on the rock and his attack will not stand. Some of you have heard the Word on giving, but you still don't do it and you wonder why you're living paycheck to

COMING UP TO LIGHT

paycheck. You have to hear it and do it to be like the wise man. The only thing that will stand is the rock which is the true teaching of the Word. This is Jesus; He is the rock. He is the Word made manifest, the Word made flesh, the Word made real, the Word of God brought into human form.

Jesus was manifested that He might destroy the works of the devil. What is He destroying? Everything Satan brings into your life. You will still go through the trial, but the difference between the one who hears and does is that when the wind blows and the storm comes, my house is still standing. When the flood rolls in, my house is still standing because I'm going to do the Word. Even if it doesn't make sense, I'm going to do it.

Paul elaborates on the idea that the construction of my house is the basis of why my house will stand, not what color I paint it or what kind of furniture I put in it. It's the foundation and the construction that will determine whether my house will stand. If I'm going through trial and tribulation and my house keeps falling—and great is the fall of it—my house didn't just fall down. If you were in a house and your house got kicked over, one neighbor saw it and they're like, "Oh man, I'm sorry about your house," great was the fall. That means your house went to toothpicks and everybody saw it. The whole country is like, "Oh my God, look at how their house fell!" Great was the fall of it. Not because of the furniture in the house, or because of the color of the house. For all intents and purposes they could have been the exact same house, just only one did the Word, and the other heard it and wouldn't do it. Dad Hagin would say it's dangerous to come up to light and then walk away. It makes perfect sense. Once I've heard, God fully expects me to do business.

Now here's the other side of this. We have to be careful because when people first come to Christ, they're learning and developing. They have bad habits, they don't understand things, and we walk them through that process of development. We take them step by step, inch by inch, line upon line, precept upon precept. We take them to the place where they can grow. People like that still have time. But what about people who have been in church for years and still act like a baby. How do you know when a baby is a baby? If there was a baby on the other side of a wall I could not see through, how would I know? Babies cry. There are babies in the Body of Christ, and we're responsible for taking care of them. But if you've been crying for years, at what point in time do you understand that the very nature of the attack you are enduring is because you heard it, but you don't do it. Light has not gained entrance and because light has not gained entrance, faith has not gained entrance. Because faith has not come, then you are wondering why you don't have any faith. You don't have any faith because you have not received the Word. If you would receive the Word as the Word has come, hear it and do it, you are likened to one who has built their house on a rock. It's the same house, same color, it could be painted beautifully, decorated extremely well, appointed with all the luxurious appointments. It could be great, but that house is coming down if you won't do what the Word has told you to do. Great will be the fall of it.

I don't know about you, but I don't like falling. Period. You know how sometimes you trip and almost fall, but nobody saw you so you catch yourself? One time I was hiking on a mountain with three other people. We were coming down—two of them in front of me, the other one beside me. As we were talking and walking, my foot literally came out from under me. In one fell swoop I went down, turned, came back up, and kept walking, so the two people in front of me never knew what happened. I would love to tell you that it was because I'm just that dexterous, but I'm not. It was my fear that I couldn't fall down in front of all these people. I'm too big to be falling on this mountain. What would have happened if I wouldn't have stopped and I kept going down? That could have been a catastrophe. So minor was the fall of that, but could you imagine what it would have been if it was great?

If you really want to see the power of God, you have to walk in light. You have to face what you don't want to face and do what you don't want to do. If you struggle with people, if you just can't stand people, you're going to have a hard time with God. Everything God did was for the people. The angels even said, "God, what is it about these two-legged creatures that You're so mindful of them?" Then you run around saying, *I don't like people. I would love ministry if it weren't for the people."*

You grow because you mature. You mature because you say, *"Wait a minute. Yeah, when I first got into Christianity I kind of struggled with this whole tithing thing."* I did, too, personally. I was doing the math. In some months I made $30,000-$40,000. "...move the decimal, carry the one...You want how much?? My wife takes half, Uncle Sam takes 28 percent, and that don't leave much left over and You want what?" I did the math, I'm just being honest. I didn't have any light on the issue. Now, however, you can't stop me. I receive gifts and figure out what they're worth and tithe off of them.

You're thinking, *Well, it don't take all that.* Maybe for you, but see, when you're believing God for all of this—the operation and the people involved in all of this—I don't have any margin of error to miss it. If I miss it, somebody else might miss it. When people's lives are dependent upon you, your margin of error changes. When you have children, you can't do what you used to do. You might have been one who said, "Woohoo! Let's all jump out of three or four airplanes at the same time!" Then you have a couple kids and you're like, "Oh, well I don't know about all of that..." You realize that you have greater responsibility. Greater responsibility brings greater light, and with greater light comes greater responsibility. You're expected to grow up.

You're in church for a long time and still can't figure out how to tithe? That's childish. Now people just coming in will have to learn. They'll have to see and test God a little bit. But if you've been around long enough to know better, then why don't you do the Word? The Word says when you get into a financial situation, sow a seed. That's what the Bible tells you to do. *"Well, I don't know, I can't."* Seriously? Let's be honest, you don't trust God. You love God, but you don't trust God. Because you don't trust Him, there's no entrance. Where there is no entrance, there is no faith. It becomes self-fulfilling.

Now you're like, *"I don't believe, I'm not sure, I don't have enough faith. I'm not there yet."* You're not there yet, so you won't allow entrance. Next thing you know you're in this big old loop and God's saying, "If you could just break this..." Those that receive may not walk in darkness. That means it's your choice.

Every area of your life in which you walk in darkness, it is your choice. If you are burning with lust and just can't keep it in your pants and thirsty as all get-out, that's you. You're burning; that's you and light has not come. The Bible tells you to never be hasty to put yourself in a relationship. You have to choose wisely. If you struggle with walking in love, faith worketh by love. If you're not able to love your enemy, your faith is being hindered. It's not even explosive, there's no power to it. You can't walk in love but then you wonder why your faith is not producing. Then

159

you have to sit through eight messages of Pastor telling you the same thing over and over again until it finally gains entrance.

Here's the difference: I'm going to keep throwing the Word at you until it beats your door down. Some of you are still holding on to the door. God's trying to get your attention. He wants to help you see that if you want to be successful in your Christian walk, you'd better learn how to spotlight and to respond to the Word. The faster you see it and do it, you will find that you will be in position all the time for blessing to come. You'll walk in it.

There are times when I have blindly walked into blessing and didn't even know it because I was just following the Holy Ghost. I wasn't quite sure how it was going to work out. "How are we going to get into a building that's eighteen thousand square feet and we've got forty people? They're telling me people are negotiating against us and they're paying a whole year's rent in cash. How's that going to happen?" I had no idea, but I'm blindly going where He's led me to go.

Obedience will put you in position to see the blessing. If your house keeps falling, then you have to check if you are following the Word. There are too many closet Christians. This is why people are struggling immensely.

"Woe unto them that call evil good, and good evil; that put darkness for light, and light for darkness; that put bitter for sweet, and sweet for bitter! Woe unto them that are wise in their own eyes, and prudent in their own sight! Woe unto them that are mighty to drink wine, and men of strength to mingle strong drink."
— *Isaiah 5:20-22*

CHOOSING LIGHT OVER DARKNESS

I had a friend of mine that I grew up with. We went to the last year of elementary school, junior high, and senior high together. We lived on the same block so we also rode the same buses. As we grew older, he was short and skinny and loved to drink. The problem was, the more he drank, the taller and bigger he got—but only in his head. We often found ourselves in situations that would potentially escalate to a place that would be slightly provocative in certain ways and would bring about the authorities. We often found ourselves speedily leaving some places and situations in order to avoid any further altercations with the local authorities. The more he mingled strong drink, the more difficult things became, the more short his attitude was, the more cocky and more arrogant. I was always the designated driver, because to be honest with you (I know all of you will be completely shocked) I never liked being out of control of myself. I like being in control of me. I always wanted to be the designated driver. If you left me or you crashed with me in the car or something happened to me on your watch, it was on and crackin'. I was one of those people who said, "Here's what I'd rather do. I'd rather not get involved in all of that, I'll be the designated driver. Everybody else can cut up. That way if they get left I'm not scared of them." Jesus said men of strength to mingle strong drink, woe unto them that are mighty to drink wine.

The expectation or the visualization of you can be altered based on wine and strong drink. Notice just before that Jesus talked about those who think they are wise and prudent in their own sight. One step further before that he said, "Be careful of those who call good, evil, and evil, good." You can be drunk with your own desire and not see truth. You can be wise in your own sight and not see truth. Because you don't see truth, you'll put a label on what's good when it's evil.

Look at how loneliness will cause a person to get into a relationship with somebody they shouldn't be in. *"Who do I talk to? Who do I have to be around? I don't have anybody, I'm by myself, I'm lonely. He might not be Mr. Right, but he'll have to be Mr. Right Now."* The problem with Mr. Right Now is he's dripping honey in your ear so now you think he's Mr. Right Eternity. Now you are in too far and then—if you have not controlled the situation well—you have crossed the lines in terms of relationships. God told you, "Don't sleep with him before you marry him," and you thought God was just trying to keep you from having fun. Now children are involved. Now it's real hard to get rid of him. Now you're stuck for the rest of your life—all because you became drunk with loneliness. You mingled strong drink and your perception of you has now changed. Now you soften the truth. *"Well, it's not that bad. He's kind of nice to me. He only beat me up once."* How do you soften? You start calling good evil and evil good. You put things that are wrong as if they were right. Now there is a shift that happens in your head because the only way you can process it is to justify why you won't tithe, why you won't support your local church, why you don't want to serve in your church... The only way you can support that is to call evil good so that you turn evil into good. You are justified by what you have done and now it feels better.

Now you become drunk because only drunk people laugh at things that aren't funny. Perhaps none of you have been around drunk people, but I have, and they laugh at things that aren't funny. They're easy to call good evil and evil good. You have to be careful that you are not drunk with yourself because you can become drunk with yourself to the point where you will call bitter sweet and sweet bitter. That's why Jesus said woe unto the person who gets this mixed up. What happens is your polarity changes. When magnets have the same polarity, they repel one another, but when they have opposite polarity, they attract one another. So if your polarity changes on one side and not the other, you will repel. Once you've reversed your polarity and reached a place where you justify what you do as okay, as many times as you hear it you still won't move. You have excuses and reasons. He said woe unto that man because you drank way too much of yourself.

"I am come a light into the world, that whosoever believeth on me should not abide in darkness. And if any man hear my words, and believe not, I judge him not; for I came not to judge the world but to save the world."
—John 12:46-47

However, the fact is, Jesus didn't come to judge, but that doesn't mean that you don't have a judge. He just said that's not going to be His job. He said, "The one who rejects me and does not receive my words has a judge. The words I have spoken will judge him on the last day." When Jesus comes in, He's light.

We've talked about the entrance of light. Just because you have light and light shows up does not mean you give entrance to light. We have been talking about this very subject of light. Light is where the Word of God becomes real in your life. When you are living in the world, you don't have much light. The Bible says you are hidden in darkness and you walk in darkness. Once you become a child of the living God, you have been translated from the kingdom of darkness into the kingdom of light. Now all of a sudden you see things clearly and you have greater understanding. As light comes, so does the attack. The more light you want to walk in, the more attack you will fall under.

People don't understand that when they first come into Christianity, they think it's going to be all bubble gum and gumdrops and sugar plums and all these other things they have somehow concocted in their own heads. They think it's easy to be a Christian, and it's not. If it was easy, everybody would do it. It takes a certain type of person with a certain type of strength and ability to endure in the faith and continue in light. The light that helped you last year is not the light that will help you this year.

This is the challenge that most people face because your problems can never be solved at the level of awareness that created them. Whatever your problems are today, you created them at a certain place. In order to overcome those problems, you are going to need a greater revelation and a greater understanding. Third John 1:2 tells us that, "Beloved, I wish above all things that thou mayest prosper and be in health, even as thy soul prospereth." Your soul is your mind, will, and emotions. If your level of healing will prosper based on only your mind prospering, then if you don't have any belief in healing you won't be healed. If you don't have any understanding of healing, you will not walk in it. What John is saying is that the level in which you will prosper, be healed, and understand will be completely predicated as your soul prospers. As your mind comes up to certain places, so will the rest of you. Now we understand the concept of why children are born headfirst. Wherever your head goes first, your body will soon follow. Everything in your life that you do, you will go in it headfirst. The thing about it is, your head is the place of the greatest battleground for your life. If you think that your greatest wrestling is in the world and in natural things, you have missed it. It is about how you think. If you think sloppy, you'll be sloppy. If you feel in your heart sloppy, you will act sloppy.

Excellence doesn't start as an outward thing, excellence comes from the inside. Some people seem to be born excellent and others are not. It's not something they were trained to do, it's something that's inside of them. If you ask me to do something, I'm going to do it 'til the wheels fall off because everything I do, I sign my signature to. If I'm going to be involved and my name is associated with it, if there's excellence in me, then excellence will come out of me. Everything that I do, I will do it headfirst.

Do you realize that your soul—your mind, will, and emotions benefit from your light? You have entrance of light to where it will change the way you think. The Bible says, "As [a man] thinketh in his heart, so is he" (Proverbs 23:7). It didn't say, "So is he is the way he thinks." The way that you think will move you either up or it'll move you down. The first place light comes is where God deals with you and talks to you about certain subjects. God says He's going to need you to let it go and deal with this, to cut some things and people out of your life, to start dealing with your flesh and not get angry all of the time, cussing people out. All these things will work in you. God is trying to change your mind. If you understand repentance, it does not mean to say you're sorry. So many people think that all they have to do is say they're sorry and then they're forgiven. Repentance in its very root comes from the word "metamorphosis" which means *to change and become something different.* If I am truly repentant, then I will turn from and go a different direction. In other words, I'll become a different person.

When we recognize that our mind will lead us places, then we get it that as a man thinketh, so is he. If I think that I'm poor, then I'll act poor. How do people behave who act poor? They're stingy. Many people won't give to God because they're stingy. No other reason. They'll write the check for cable in a heartbeat. Can't let their internet be shut down for a day. Good Lord, you're about to lose your ever-lovin' mind. It's interesting that we have our priorities certain ways and we think God's okay with it because, *after all, He knows my heart,* which is exactly why we should be concerned because He sees through the softener you've given yourself.

How your mind prospers, how you think about certain things, will determine what you are. If you have a problem with submission, for example, you'll struggle with being promoted and growing because you'll always be thinking, *"If I'm submissive, then they'll take advantage of me."* Here's the problem: When I looked at my parents I submitted to them. If I did not submit to them, they would apply a certain amount of pressure to my gluteus maximus until my cerebral cortex began to get a new revelation. I did not think they were taking advantage of me. I thought they were protecting me and loving me. I thought that love meant that which was in my best interest would be done by those who loved me even if I didn't know better.

It's bizarre how submission has become one of those things where we think we'll be hurt and taken advantage of. The truth of the matter is sometimes we will. The Bible says that if somebody does take advantage of you and you have done it unto Him, He will repay both them and you. Now, it becomes smarter for me to learn how to submit. That way the burden is not on me, it's on the one I've submitted to. Should they mess up, they'll have to deal with the Lord. I know I will be repaid.

Any time you are struggling with something God told you to do, it's because the darkness in you comprehends it not. If you knew the benefit and understood the realities of it, why would you not do it? Years ago when I was in sales, my personal philosophy was not that I was going to sell you. I didn't use hard-core selling techniques and step-down closes and Benjamin Franklin closes. I wasn't a hard closer. I came to a belief a long time ago that if I educate you to know what I know, then you'll do it. If I can't give you good information to help you make a decision, then I don't need to sell you anyway. I'm not trying to sell you, I'm trying to help you and I would never sell anything I didn't believe in. The reality of that for me was, if I educate you, smart people make smart decisions. Dumb people make dumb decisions. My only responsibility is to make sure I stay on the end of the smart decision.

Why don't we understand it's the same thing with light? My job is not to beat you over the head and force you to do anything, although it may feel like that sometimes. My job is to educate you in the way God wants it done. You can do it any way you want to. You can live this life any way you choose.

The struggle is real for you, but my reality is my Word tells me that everywhere I go, I am surrounded with favor as with a shield. So when I show up, help shows up. When I step in, help comes in. When I know the kingdom of God is on the inside of me, then wherever I go, the kingdom has also arrived and I am surrounded with favor. People are looking to do something extra for me. It isn't fair and I don't care. The problem is, the people who say it's not fair are on the other end of it. Favor is not fair. God is not fair, God is just. *"Why should he walk in that and I don't?"* Because he gives, supports, and serves and you won't. If you can't see why that's important, then that's why you're struggling. Somewhere along the line he got some light and walked in it. This is where the rubber hits the road. Many have been in church and heard it over and over but they still won't do it. We'll walk out of here today and those of you who know what you're supposed to do, you still won't do it because you're thinking I'm talking to the person next to you—when the reality is I'm talking to you. Why? Not that I need anything from you, I couldn't care less. You don't believe tithing works? Go tithe to the church down the street. Pick one. As God blesses you and you start to see it, bring it back here so we can use it and do what we have to do in the house where you're getting fed. How many pastors would tell you to do that?

I know God works. I have light and I walk in it. If you make the decision to do it God's way, then you will need light on the matter. Any issue you are struggling with, you're wrestling with darkness, not light. When light shows up, light comes to help. I don't know why you would even think that if you are in total darkness, and if somebody shows up with a flashlight, that's help. Jesus said He is the light and anybody who believes in Him should not/may not abide in darkness. That implies that even when He shows up and brings light, you still could stay in darkness. It's your choice. Faith cometh by hearing and hearing by the Word of God. Light shows up that way, but light is not received that way. Just because light shows up—and it's been explained and shown to you in the Bible over and over again—does not necessarily mean that you're going to accept it. The fact that you won't do it is a sign that you are still wrestling with darkness when you have been translated into the kingdom of light.

Here's what people do. They can't stand what's not familiar. It isn't that God is difficult; it's that God is not intuitive to you. There are times we'll have situations that occur and one of the questions we always ask is, is it hard or is it just counterintuitive? To say it's hard is one thing, to say it's counterintuitive is another. Hard means that it's physically difficult. Counterintuitive means we're not used to doing it that way. Plenty of things are not hard, but they are counterintuitive. Because they're counterintuitive, your soul has not prospered.

CHOOSING LIGHT OVER DARKNESS

Do you realize that the stupidity that's in your brain is what trips you up all of the time? It's not just yours, it's mine too. I have made it a personal mission to eradicate as much stupidity in my head that I can by beginning to consume as much light as I can because light always removes darkness. If you have a problem with people always irritating you, then you need to learn how to disconnect the button. If you think they should just stop doing stupid stuff, good luck with that.

Years ago, I worked for a computer company and one day, all of a sudden the front manager burst into my office to tell me the cops were there. I went to the front of the store, and I'm telling you it looked like Starsky and Hutch. There were probably seven or eight police cars in the parking lot all caddywhompus and the officers all jumped out. One of them came in with his hand on his gun and yells, "What's going on here?" I'm like, "You tell me!"

Turns out, I had a friend of mine who couldn't find a babysitter for her son and asked me if I could watch him for the day so I brought him to work with me. Under the front counter, he happened to see a little red button that, evidently in his mind, was just begging to be pressed. That red button, unbeknown to him, was a panic alarm that went straight to the police department saying we were being held up.

The cop is asking me what's going on, I'm asking him what's going on, then he asks me if I have an ID and all that stuff. I showed him my ID and business cards and we got it all clear that I'm the right person. He then asked, "Okay, what's the panic alarm about?" I said, "What panic alarm?" He said, "We received an alarm saying that you guys were being robbed." I said, "We are not being robbed, number one. Number two, we didn't push any panic alarm." He went out, got on the radio, commanded dispatch and let them all know, and they all bolted just as fast as they came in. Something then said to me, "Ask the little man." So I went into my office and said, "Let me ask you a question. Did you see a little red button anywhere in here?" He nodded. I said, "Could you show it to me?" He took me right to the counter. I said, "Did you push this?" He nodded again.

Here's the point I'm trying to make: He's a child, he saw a red button, he pushed it. That's what children do. You, on the other hand, walk around with this big red button because your attitude stinks. I've learned that I'm not going to let you push my button. Instead, here's what I'm going to do. At times I may still have this blinking, but I'm going to snip the wires behind it so even if you come up to me and start pressing the button, the response from me is going to be, "Everything is going to be all right." Some of you are so tied to that button that you can't see the power of God in your life because you're too flesh-ruled. So now every time you get close to the things of God, Satan comes in and he hits the button. And as soon as he hits the button, you have a problem.

These are the challenges that people really face. Some of you know that I'm talking about you. You are two seconds from coming in hot. If we can really be honest, it's childish. Jesus said, "The way you'll know these people are Mine is by their love." *"Well, I can't stand so-and-so, they're always smiling and laughing and talking about love. They're just fake."* No, you're fake. The reason you're fake and they're not is because they are His disciples. We know this by the love they have for their brethren. I can drink diesel, smoke like a chimney, and sleep in a garage, but that doesn't make me a Mack Truck. People can come into church, they can shout, they can hoop, they can holler, but that doesn't make them Christian. This is the place where God's expecting us to step up.

You've been a baby sucking on your thumb long enough. If you keep sucking on it, you're going to end up with buck teeth. The problem is, we get so bent out of shape as God deals with us on certain areas because darkness has become intuitive. We've lived in darkness for so long. It's intuitive that when we get into a financial situation, we have to work more jobs because that's what men do. We solve problems! If He promised me that He'd never leave me nor forsake me, then I know that if I'm doing what He's asked me to do and other things are not working correctly, then it is not my responsibility to work harder. My responsibility is to get into the Word and figure out what adjustments I have to make.

"Wherefore, he saith, Awake thou that sleepest, and arise from the dead, and Christ shall give thee light. See, then, that ye walk circumspectly, not as fools but as wise, Redeeming the time, because the days are evil. Wherefore, be ye not unwise but understanding what the will of the Lord is."
—Ephesians 5:14-17

The first thing you have to do is wake up. Paul is not speaking to people who are dead; that would be silly. He's not talking to someone in a coffin. He's speaking to people who are alive. He's not speaking to awake you out of natural sleep, but spiritual sleep. If you would awaken out of spiritual sleep, then Christ would give you light. Notice that it's not automatic that when Christ gives you light that you will walk as wise. People think that because the Word came, they are wise because they have knowledge.

I had a recruiter in high school who was a really cool guy. He'd talk real gruff and say, "Boy, knowledge is power!" He had me convinced of this, but knowledge is *not* power. Wisdom, the application of knowledge, is power. I can know what to do and still not do it. I can know the answer and still not get it. Therefore, having knowledge is not power. The ability to apply what I know brings the power. Just because light shows up, power is not automatically imputed. Light shows up and power shows up but it is not yours until you apply it with wisdom. That's why Paul says when Christ shows up, He'll give you light. Then, make sure that you walk circumspectly. This means to walk constantly while evaluating circularly everything around you to make sure you know you are not missing it in certain places and areas of your life. As you walk circumspectly, he also says don't walk as a fool because fools hear the Word but won't do the Word. A fool is somebody who knows but won't do.

Let me pass on an education Pastor Ricky gave to me. He said there's a difference between being stupid and being ignorant. Ignorant, you don't know; stupid is you know and you won't do. "See that you walk circumspectly, not as fools, but as wise." In your wisdom you will redeem the time. You could be unwise, you could be stupid, walk in darkness and be a fool, but he says see that you don't do that. When Christ gives you light, the power in the light is based on your ability to walk in it. That's where you now redeem the time.

It took me five years of church to figure out that tithing is a supernatural thing and that it doesn't match up with my natural understanding. My little head cannot comprehend why it works or how it works, but there are umpteen people I could think of right now who can tell me that it works. If I've ignored it for five years, I'm not walking in light. The moment that I get it, if I walk in it—although for the first five years I might struggle financially—the moment I get it, God said if I'd just do it, He'll redeem the time. He will bring back what I should have had and He'll do it in a way that's supernatural and faster than you ever could have done by yourself.

All of a sudden people start walking in things when it comes to them. When it first happens, you feel uncomfortable. You're almost ashamed to tell people you were blessed because you don't want them getting jealous, angry, or mad. Haters is the breakfast of champions, but I don't want that breakfast too often because haters come with their own set of challenges and problems. Then you get to a point where you're like, *"It is what it is. My God is well able to do exceedingly abundant more than I can ask or think."* I could ask for a lot, but I couldn't care less how other people feel.

You go through stages because more light comes and you think, *"Wait a minute, I don't need to feel guilty. God's blessing me because I'm obedient."* You ever have more than one child? One child is very obedient and the other one isn't. If we want to be honest that changes from time to time. It isn't that you love one more than the other, it's that it's easier to deal with the obedient one. People are disobedient toward God, then they think, *"Well, God doesn't like me."* You're right; God doesn't like you. He loves you and He loved you first which means He doesn't need you to love Him.

You know how it is when you get into a relationship. You first start dating, you're in the infatuation stage, and you think, *"I think I love this girl but I can't tell her."* At the same time she's thinking, *"You know, I think I love this dude, but I can't tell him yet. Not enough time has gone by. He's going to think I'm a creeper."* You're right, he will. Isn't it funny how people don't want to say it first, but God comes out and said He loved you first. Whether you love Him or not, whether you think He's a creeper or not, whether you feel any kind of way about it or not, doesn't matter. He loves you. If He loves you first, then why don't you understand that it's His desire to be a blessing to you? When you're swinging from the chandeliers all the time, it doesn't change that He loves you, you're just hard to bless.

When you become hard to bless because you're hard-headed, what are you blaming God for? It's not like He doesn't desire to bless you, but if you don't know the combination, you'll be sitting at your locker spinning the dial, wondering why this thing isn't opening. It's because you don't understand God requires obedience. Obedient children seem to be rewarded more. Now when Child A is sitting enjoying an ice cream cone and Child B doesn't get one because they were acting up, Child B has no right to be mad at Child A because Child A did what they were supposed to.

Paul says, "...redeeming the time because the days are evil." Life drifts towards complexity. I don't care who you are or what nationality you are. The older you grow, the crazier life becomes. I originally thought when I was in my teens, if I could just grow up, but with every passing year I realize growing up is overrated. However, it sure beats the alternative. You think about growing up as a way of getting freedom and intellect, then you reach a certain point where you're like, *"I still don't know this yet and I still haven't figured it out. Why can't I seem to get these answers?"* Then God steps in and you think, "Yes! I'm going to understand everything!" Then He flips it upside down and you're still trying to figure it out.

Life drifts towards complexity. Things become harder, they don't get easier. Because of that, He's telling you the days are evil. The days are not working for you, they're working against you so you're going to need to redeem the time. The only way to do that is to be wise. Now through wisdom, what it takes you five years to do, I can do it in one. The sign of the anointing is I can do more with less. I don't need to make as much money as you to live better than you. Folks say, *"You see how Pastor dressed? You see all the stuff he got? You see the car he drives? The house he lives in?"* They go down the list and they think I must be making a fortune. I'm blessed.

This is what people struggle with before they don't have light. When more light comes, more blessing comes. How do you supernaturally deal with things that were designed to hold you back, then all of a sudden God steps into the middle of the situation and He turns it all around. He might not have brought you more money, but He might have changed the circumstance. He might have made a way when there was no way. He might have moved when you thought it wasn't going to work. He might have gone to the banker and said, "Hey, give it to them." There are things that happen that God is doing. If you have God on your side, who can be against you? I'm not talking about money, I'm talking about light. I don't need more money, what I need is more light, understanding, direction, and God.

"Now a certain man was sick, named Lazarus, of Bethany, the town of Mary and her sister Martha. (It was that Mary who anointed the Lord with ointment, and wiped his feet with her hair, whose brother Lazarus was sick.) Therefore his sisters sent unto him, saying, Lord, behold, he whom thou lovest is sick. When Jesus heard that, he said, This sickness is not unto death, but for the glory of God, that the Son of God might be glorified by it. Now Jesus loved Martha, and her sister, and Lazarus. When he had heard, therefore, that he was sick, he abode two days still in the same place where he

175

was. Then, after that, saith he to his disciples, Let us go into Judaea again. His disciples say unto him, Master, the Jews of late sought to stone thee; and goest thou there again?"
—John 11:1-8

If I told you I was I sick and I needed you to come to me but you stayed away two extra days, it's only natural that I'd question whether you loved me or not. *This dude's talking about how much he loved me, I send somebody to say I'm sick unto death. He's talking about how he has to hang out over there a couple more days, then he'll come see me.* Jesus said, "This sickness is not unto death, but for the glory of God."

Can you imagine? He gets word that Lazarus is sick. We know He loves Lazarus as He's made that confession, yet he stays two more days. After the second day, He's like, "Come on, let's go." The disciples said, "Wait a minute, we like the two days. We thought you forgot about that. We were hoping you weren't going to do that." Jesus says something that is so different in His response to them. He answered and said, "Are there not twelve hours in a day?" To me, that's like, "Hey, can you come pray for my sick friend in the hospital?" and I ask you, "Is there enough cream in your coffee?"

He says, "If any man walk in the day, he stumbleth not because he seeth the light of this world. But if a man walk in the night, he stumbleth because there is no light in him" (John 11:9-10). In other words, Jesus explains to them He's being led by light. He already said the sickness is not unto death, and if He's not there to judge them but His Word will judge them, then every word that He has spoken, that word must come to pass. If the word must come to pass, then the thing that'll judge is the Word because the Word will stand true. The Bible says that the Word will not return unto Him void but it shall accomplish that which it was sent to do (Isaiah 55:11).

"Aren't there twelve hours in a day?" I know if I set out at dawn, I have twelve hours before it gets dark. That's two issues that have to be faced—light and time. If I have a certain amount of time and I have a certain amount of light, then I have a certain amount of window to accomplish whatever it is for God's plan for me to accomplish. So when He asked, "Are there not twelve hours in the day?", He was helping them—and me—to understand that as long as I am in light, then I still have time. However, if I'm not walking in light, I'm walking in darkness. This is why man stumbles.

If I am constantly tripping up over myself, then what I have to recognize is that I am not walking in light. What area in my circumspect life am I looking at to say if I keep tripping up, somewhere darkness is pervading into my life and this is why I keep stumbling? Jesus said even if they came to stone me, even if I'm walking in light, even if a problem is coming near me, even if the storm is raging against me, if I am walking in light then God will turn that storm and it will miss me. There's no way if I'm walking in light that anything waged against me will be successful. There are twelve hours left in the day and if I stay in it, I don't have to be afraid.

So many people struggle with being afraid and it's because they're walking in darkness. They know in darkness they're going to stumble. It's not an *if*, it's a *when*. God comes along and says, "Okay, let Me give you the solution. You don't have to be afraid, just walk in light." He who says he has fellowship with God will walk in light with Him and he will do light, but he who says he has fellowship with God yet does dark things is a liar and the truth is not in him. Once you understand what Jesus was telling them, He said, "Look, are there not twelve hours left in the day?", then that means as long as you walk in light, you will not stumble. Some of you live in such a place that when people in your life make demands, you jump. It gives no room for God. Just because you have a need does not mean I have to fill it.

Satan will use things, family, and other people to draw on you to bring you to a place where you can't even breathe anymore. He does it to so many people. We think we have to go, but Jesus hung out for two more days. As we read the rest of the story, Jesus hung out for two more days because He wanted to make sure old dude was dead. By the time He got there, Lazarus had been dead four days. They didn't have the same processes we have. The Bible says he was dead and stinking. Jesus needed him to be good and dead. If He had shown up while His friend was in his sick bed and he got healed off a sick bed, that might have been a little bit of a miracle and people might have said, "That was great! Jesus healed him." But if he's dead, stinking and decomposing, and Jesus stands before the tomb and says, "Lazarus come forth!", all of a sudden you see him coming out of the tomb.

I know you're all full of faith and power, but I'm going to be honest with you. I'd stand there to see what was going down. I would have been there when he yelled "Lazarus!" *Huh, let me see this!* I'm not going to lie, when I'd hear him coming up out of that thing, I'd have been like, "Oh no. I have to go..." I know Lazarus has been in there for a minute. He's decomposing. Let's just say he was slightly alive as he hasn't eaten in three days, he's been sealed up. So if he wasn't dead and all of a sudden I hear footsteps, I'd have been like, "Peace!" When the news got to Him, with the bad news came light. He said the sickness is not unto death. How would he have known that if in the midst of the situation light didn't come with it?

Every situation that happens in your life, light comes with it. God doesn't allow you to be tempted without opening a window. He doesn't give you anything more than what you can handle. Yet, Jesus was so sensitive to light that when the problem came, so did the answer. What He spoke was not the problem, He spoke the answer. They spoke the problem and He said the sickness is not unto death.

Here's the problem: Did Lazarus die? Yes. Did he stay that way? No. It might look like something in our life is going to die. It might look like it went a certain way, it might actually die, but God can redeem the time. He can take it back to where it used to be and set everything back in order. To God, time means nothing. Time means something to you, but it means nothing to Him. He could start from the beginning or the end and flip it all upside down because He's God. He says, "I don't need to worry about this because I walk in light."

So many people are struggling because they won't walk in light. They're walking in darkness and they're expecting something. The definition of insanity is simple: It's doing the same thing over and over again expecting a different result. The reality is that if you live the way you used to live in the world, then go back to that. If any of you have ever come to the realization that the way you lived in the world was not what you wanted, the things you found yourself in the middle of were not what you wanted, when you woke up in places and you weren't quite sure exactly where you were, and it was not what you wanted, the lifestyle that you used to live was not what you wanted and you come to the end of yourself, you realize you need light to move out of the darkness, because you don't want the darkness anymore.

The truth of the matter is, if you cannot comprehend light, you are walking in darkness and you need to walk in light. The only way to walk in light is you must allow your mind to start changing. You have to gain a new understanding of things. I can't tell you how many times men will say, "Oh, I've *got* to take my wife out to dinner." And I'll say, "You mean you *get* to take your wife to dinner." You need to start thinking back to the days when you were rockin' bellbottoms with the butterfly collar up in the club talking about, "Watch out tonight, girl!" You didn't have anybody and you went home and slept by yourself. You were wishing you had a wife, now you have one. You see the line of thinking? "I have to" means it's an obligation; "I get to" means it's a privilege. I love date night; my wife is dressed finer than a mug. I put her on my arm and it's on like Donkey Kong. I've changed my thinking. It's a small price to pay to see a smile on her face.

When you think differently, you do differently. That's why John said, "Beloved, I wish above all things that thou mayest prosper and be in health, even as thy soul prospereth" (3 John 1:2). If there are three things I want you to do, but I say "above all else," which one do you think is the more important? The one I'm about to say "above all else." Do you realize the greatest battle you will ever fight is in your mind? This is the place where light is trying to gain entrance and your mind oftentimes is rejecting it. It's like, *"No, I wasn't taught that way. I was raised that you just don't go to church. I was taught God is not a healer. My grandmother died; she was very religious but she still died anyway. So I can't believe God is a healer because if He is, why did He let her die?"*

CHOOSING LIGHT OVER DARKNESS

This is how some people think when darkness pervades their mind. When light comes and you say, "God is a healer," they're like *"Oh, that wasn't for me."* Why isn't it that for you? *"Because I've had experiences."* I don't care about your experiences, light is coming. How do you deal with light? *"I'm just not into that giving stuff."* Okay, stay in poverty. *"Well, I do all right."* Then imagine what you could do if God was in it. If you want what you can do, that's fine. I've been all I can be and it just wasn't enough so I'm okay with supernatural assistance. I'm okay with knowing that when I have a need I can take it to my Father and say, "This is what I need," and somehow He just moves things around. Next thing I know, I'm just the benefactor. I'm okay with that. If you like working hard, go for it, but when you're ready, I have light for you.

The word is full of light and if I can help you to see just one more thing, we'll take a step. When I've seen people take steps, I've seen them start tithing and their whole family shifts. I've seen people who start walking in love and all of a sudden things just start happening. You say, *"What does walking in love have to do with me getting my finances together?"* You can tithe all you want to, but if you don't walk in love, you'll never prosper. If you won't walk in love, you might as well keep your tithe because you can't pay God. See how that works? Areas that you think have nothing to do with each other have everything to do with each other and it's all about you walking in light. That's why John said be circumspect. What are the areas? If you're struggling with finances, then that's an area you need some light on. Sit down with some people and say, "I know I'm being hard-headed, but help me." If it's my love walk, I might have to sit down with some people and say, "Do me a favor. Talk to me about walking in love because I just can't seem to move past this. Every time so-and-so presses my button I get angry and I'm ready to whoop." Well, the love of God should constrain you; that's what the Bible says. Faith works by love; your faith won't work if your love walk doesn't work. Some of you become so angry and bent out of shape, you're walking in the flesh all the time and you're wondering why your faith doesn't work. Then you're blaming God.

Some of you, because you're not wise with your money and stewardship, are not prospering and then you're asking God. I don't care how many times you come up here and have somebody lay hands on you. We can lay hands on you until we rub the hair smooth off your head, but if you are not wise with your stewardship, you will not prosper. When it comes to healing, you can't keep your confession straight. You're in here talking about "Child, I'm healed!" but as soon as you walk out of here and the doctor asks how you feel today, you're like, "I'm sick as a dog." You go around telling everybody how you feel because you love the sympathy it brings. You want everybody to connect with you on an emotional level. I don't need anybody to connect with me, I'm fine, I'm lovely. Everything in my body is the way it's supposed to work from the top of my head to the soles of my feet. I feel great. *"You don't look great."* That's an opinion.

The thing about it is this: If we're going to walk in light, we have to recognize that he who walks in light doesn't stumble because light is there. That's what Jesus was telling them. There are no mistakes when there's light, as long as you follow what you're told. I've watched people in their relationships. God told them not to mess with someone and leave them alone, but they go barreling over the cliff. Or one week it's "Leave them alone" and the next week it's "God told me to go ahead." Did He now? Is He slightly schizophrenic? What changed in the God that says, "I change not"?

CHOOSING LIGHT OVER DARKNESS

Light will cause you not to stumble and every time you stumble, every time I have stumbled, it's because I've allowed darkness to rule my footsteps. As darkness rules my footsteps, then how could His Word be a light unto my feet and a lamp unto my path? If His Word is a light unto where I'm supposed to go, then I recognize that He is my ultimate source of light. As I trust in Him, I trust in His Word. It's the entrance of His Word that brings light. His Word is light, but His Word is not bringing light. It's the *entrance* of His Word, the way you allow it to come in and change the way you think.

Your mind gets around this stuff and you say, *"Wait a minute, God says I've still have to love you. I want to smack, punch, and cuss you out. However, I'm going to step back because the love of God constrains me and I'm going to love you anyway."* That's what He means when light has entrance. It means that no matter how you feel, you still do the Word. If you want to make your way successful, then you'd better learn how to disconnect from your feelers because your feelers will allow you to do things. Your feelers will cause you to do things. Your feelers will drive you places that you should not go. If you would stay with the Word and give the Word first place, then every time you are faced with the decision of darkness or light, you'll choose light. When you choose light, you will not stumble.

I was watching a show about a group of preachers in a particular city and one of the preacher's daughters said to another preacher's daughter, "The first thing I need in a man is he's got to be godly." The other girl said, "My husband isn't a believer, I don't agree." Now, you're a preacher's child, so that means you know what the Word says, but you're sitting here saying you don't believe...so I'll be curious to see how that's all going to pan out. However, how great does darkness have to be to override what is so very clear? Be not unequally yoked. How does that work? This is where light has come. One has received it, the other one hasn't. Now they're going to bear the fruit of that. However, if I walk in light, I will not stumble. I just can't. It'll always make my way successful.

That doesn't mean I won't have problems, challenges, or miss part of the light. I might retain only a little bit but God needs me to have more. So I might slightly stumble, but if I'm walking in the fullness of the light God has for me then I'll never stumble. Why? Because there are twelve hours in a day. With every piece of light comes that twelve hours to walk in it, but God forbid if I'm slow. Some of you, that's your problem. You have light but you're slow and you don't realize there are only twelve hours. You are at the thirteenth hour now getting around to it.

A guy I worked for in high school had a little round wooden coin with TUIT written on it. I saw this little coin and I said, "What is that?" He said, "It's a round tuit. I'll do something when I get 'around to it.'" People are always messing around waiting. Remember, there are twelve hours. Jesus didn't say they weren't going to get me, He said they just can't get me while I'm walking in light. There will come a time when darkness and night has to come, but it won't be right now.